INSIDE THE RAFALUTION

MARK DOUGLAS

For Jen – my rock.
Without your patience, support and love,
this would not have been possible.

First published in Great Britain and Ireland in 2017 by
Trinity Mirror Sport Media, PO Box 48, Old Hall Street, Liverpool L69 3EB.

www.tmsportmedia.com
@SportMediaTM

Trinity Mirror Sport Media is a part of Trinity Mirror plc.
One Canada Square, Canary Wharf, London, E15 5AP.

1

Paperback ISBN: 978-1-910335-76-5
eBook ISBN 978-1-908319-79-1

Book editing & production: James Cleary
Jacket design: Rick Cooke

Printed and bound by CPI Group (UK) Ltd, Croydon, CR0 4YY.

Contents

Contents

Acknowledgements

IT was about 10 to nine in the evening when my phone rang. The number that flashed up had only been punched in a few days before so it was a bit of a surprise to see Joe Kinnear calling.

A gruff voice on the other end. "Hello. Is that Mark from the *Journal*? I want to tell you what's going to happen tomorrow. I've had nothing but sh*t from the press since I've come to the club so I'm going to let them have it."

Kinnear chuckled to himself. The conversation went on for another 45 minutes, Kinnear unburdening himself about what he thought about journalism, journalists and the media. To a journalist. I told him he'd be better off building bridges. Newcastle United in 2008 was a powder keg. Kevin Keegan had walked, as his replacement there was work to do to try and salvage a season that had been ruined by in-fighting and mistrust. His appointment was only supposed to be for six weeks: surely there were more important things to do?

He wasn't listening. The next day he gave the press conference that everyone remembers. He swore 52 times that afternoon. When he finally left, there was complete silence. This was Newcastle United under Mike Ashley.

To understand what Rafa Benitez has done for Newcastle, you need to know where it was. It hasn't always been as chaotic or undignified as it was under Kinnear in that first spell but the tendency for the club to vacillate wildly between outrage and optimism makes it volatile. It is a city that loves its football club and there is a yearning for it to represent all the best things about Newcastle: it's friendliness, warmth, creativity and pride.

The wrong characters had been involved with it for a long time before Benitez arrived and its reputation had been trashed by some of them. None of that helped the lazy and infuriating idea that Newcastle was an impetuous, expectant and impossible club that no-one could manage.

The crises were one thing. The worst thing to witness in the years before Benitez was the way the club had started to actively dampen the expectations of its supporters. You will read here that a key philosophy of the club before Benitez was to be the best it could be "pound for pound", a dreadful catchphrase supposed to represent a desire to punch above its weight but actually signifying a move towards a cold, hollow club that had given up on inspiration or ambition.

Benitez changed that in an instant. He is the most qualified manager the club has had since Sir Bobby Robson – and many would say his CV is even better. He represented such a shift in thinking from the club that it still seems impossible that they turned to him when they did, or that he accepted it. In a world where top managers can often be self-serving and driven by preserving their own reputation, here was a genuinely world-class character prepared to take a job that had defeated so many before him. It was just a perfect story.

What he did on and off the pitch after taking over also speaks of a man who worked quickly to gain an understanding of the club and his surroundings. He took lessons from the club's historian, visited the city's monuments and worked closely with the communities. Hopefully some of the stories in this book illustrate the changes he made – and the impact that he had.

ACKNOWLEDGEMENTS

It has been an uplifting year to cover Newcastle United and I am indebted to all of my colleagues at *The Chronicle* and *Journal* for their help over the course of the season.

Thanks to Steve Hanrahan at Trinity Mirror Sport Media for taking a chance on the book, to Lewis Arnold for the cover shot and to Chris Waugh and Stu Jamieson for their proof reading expertise and suggestions.

For the interviews with Benitez's backroom staff, I owe a debt of gratitude to Newcastle United's Wendy Taylor and Ryan Parrish. It was a particularly fascinating day spent in their company. Dan King and Lee Marshall from the club have also been a help.

I would like to thank everyone who agreed to be interviewed for this book: Alex Hurst of Gallowgate Flags, Steve Farrell, Liz Luff at the incredible Sir Bobby Robson Foundation and the many others.

My family and friends offered invaluable advice. My father, Kevin, in particular, was a fantastic sounding board along with my mother, Sue. Steve Adcock was great support.

Most of all I am indebted to my amazing wife, Jen, who provided such an incredible support during the writing process. I could not have done it without her.

Mark Douglas, May 2017

Foreword

by Mick Quinn
(57 goals in 110 games for Newcastle United)

THE two cities where Rafa Benitez has felt most at home – perhaps even more than in Madrid, where he was born – are Liverpool and Newcastle.

I can understand that. I was born in Liverpool and it's where I learned my values but Newcastle, where I had the fortune to play in the number nine shirt, is just as much home to me.

I'd come from Portsmouth, down on the south coast, and I loved playing there. But when I signed for Newcastle and drove to the city, I knew from the first minute I arrived that it was the right move. The way people talked to you, the love that you felt: it was so similar to Liverpool. Newcastle were going through a torrid time. The fans were at war with the board but the affection for the club hadn't diminished. The first week I was there I went to a barbers in Gosforth to get my hair cut and it was like we spoke the same language: football, laughter. I felt it.

I think that's why Rafa came to Newcastle and why he stayed. When they announced Rafa as manager I had to pinch myself. The idea that he would join Newcastle felt so far-fetched – they were a club that had specialised in making problems for themselves but here they were, appointing one of the most decorated managers of his age. Newcastle were just desperate for a big name, someone who could come in with the charisma and personality that Rafa has to make sure things were done right. He brought knowledge and he won the supporters round in an instant.

You can see from some of the stories about the little things he's done – the community events, the charities, what he has said to people – that he is a man who understands the importance of Newcastle to the city. And it also helps that he's a fantastic football manager, too. I've met him a few times and you are always so impressed by what he says and does about football.

I was lucky to be part of Newcastle when they were on the upward curve, promoted from the Second Division, and the city is just amazing when the club is doing well. There is such a buzz around the place that you feel 10 foot tall as a player. When I go back now, I feel the same thing. I think Newcastle, united, are a force to be reckoned with and if the manager can keep going at the same rate, there's no reason why they can't keep being successful and hope for much greater things.

One thing that has stuck with me is the way Rafa looked when Newcastle lifted that Championship trophy. He has won the Champions League, La Liga, the FA Cup, the Europa League – all of these huge competitions where he's jostling with the world's best. But his smile after they won that title was as wide as the River Tyne. He looked just as satisfied and pleased as he did when he won the really big trophies with Liverpool, Valencia and Chelsea.

This is a world-class manager whose methods have brought him success wherever he goes. He has re-invigorated Newcastle and the story behind it is a fascinating one.

Prologue

"Having this city behind you means everything. They should be a top team"

Rafa Benitez, April 24, 2017

RAFA BENITEZ prowled the touchline, his agitated manner betraying his frustration. There was a frenzy about the Newcastle United manager as he cajoled his players – an exasperation at every misplaced pass or fractionally mistimed run. He pointed to Matt Ritchie, his player of the season, and gestured to him to move four yards to the right to offer a better angle for the impending throw-in.

Newcastle were three goals to the good and a man up on mid-table Preston North End and Benitez's team, pieced together after the most bruising of relegations, were just 15 minutes away from delivering instant promotion redemption at a raucous St James' Park. But the manager could not settle in his seat or drink it in. Even now, with this gruelling, marathon promotion race almost run, Benitez felt he had work to do. The zeal of the obsessive perfectionist had driven him from the moment relegation was confirmed – the indignity heaped on Newcastle while the players sat in their front rooms, helpless as arch-rivals Sunderland swept aside Everton – and it did not desert him at this point.

Ritchie looked over and understood. He moved and received the ball, angling a pass into the path of Yoan Gouffran. Benitez nodded, turning to the coaching staff to deliver instructions to substitute Jack Colback. The Tyneside air felt bitterly cold but on a patch of grass at St James' Park, there was enough furious, nervous energy being generated to heat up the grand old stadium.

***

WHEN the final whistle went, and Newcastle United were upgraded from Championship to Premier League status less than a year after their demotion had been confirmed, Benitez's demeanour changed, too.

Newcastle's manager was once asked why he did not celebrate goals during matches and replied, matter-of-factly, that he felt this was the perfect time to deliver instructions to his players. His inquisitor may as well have been asking the Spaniard why he always wore shoes. For Benitez, it sometimes feels like the joy is in the process – working out ways to solve problems rather than reaping the rewards of actually overcoming them.

But this was different. Newcastle's promotion had been expected. To the outside world they had swaggered into the Championship with the look of a winner, the shortest-priced favourites in the history of the division. It had not worked out that way, Benitez having to summon all the tricks of his managerial craft to guide a listing ship through the division's surprisingly choppy waters. That he had done it with a club that was riddled with leaks and riven by dissatisfaction just a year before made it more satisfying to the man who – finally – celebrated with the enthusiasm of the sell-out home crowd.

He punched the air, the first time he had done that in a year in the job. Turning to the bench, there was a word of thanks to the row of backroom staff that had been there every step of the way. Then he turned and shook hands with fans behind the dug-out. The grinning coaching staff stood, somewhat sheepishly, at the request of Newcastle's club photographer, Serena Taylor. There was a ruffle of her hair, and a kiss on the cheek. Benitez flashed a thumbs up to the crowd. He wanted there to be pictures that represented what this was: a collective effort, a triumph of a group of men who believed, absolutely, in what they were doing and threw their energy into it.

Then Benitez headed for the centre circle, seeking out every one of the 18 players who were part of the squad that had carried them to the 4-1 win over Preston that had sealed promotion. Then the slow, impromptu victory lap took him to the ground staff, bunching up the goal nets in front of the Gallowgate End – still packed full, mercifully shorn of the usual gaps of seats contributed by the early leavers rushing for Metros or to beat the car park rush. This was standing room only: the perfect chance to catch the ultimate smart phone footage of a candid Benitez celebration.

There was a thumbs up to the people who had invested in him. Another raised fist. Then applause, pointing to the stands. Ritchie Vallens' *La Bamba*, the Rafa anthem, was blasting out from the speakers. A ground that two years before had been deserted by its people revelled in the rebirth.

***

BACK in the tunnel that snakes out from the old Milburn reception at St James' Park, Benitez gathered the rest of the staff for a picture. This was a bigger photo: he cajoled kit man Neil

Stoker into the portrait, club doctor Paul Catterson was also in the extended shot. There were smiles.

Benitez and his team had surprised English football by agreeing to the assignment of lifting Newcastle United out of the Championship. His arrival had preceded relegation, of course, but he could have walked away without a blemish on his CV. Certainly few supporters would have laid the blame for beating a quick retreat at his door. That failure was not his to wallow in.

When he did agree to it – powered by the emotion of a support who believed in him completely – Benitez effectively signed over his life to the cause. That is what you get with this manager: straining every sinew, expending ever spare minute, cajoling every single person he encounters to make things as good as they can possibly be. At a club like Newcastle – that had grown tired at years of neglect – managing can be an excruciatingly uncomfortable experience. Many had turned away from it, or been beaten by it. But Benitez confronted it and channelled the yearning into a season to be proud of.

There was no other way for him than promotion. Having sat in on the meetings, he will have known the dire consequences of a prolonged stay in the foothills of the Championship for a club of Newcastle's means. Failing to go up would have been more than a personal disappointment, it would have meant profound challenges for a club that would have had to cut its cloth like the rest of the fallen giants. Given the way Benitez had been embraced by Newcastle fans, he did not wear that burden lightly. It chipped away at him when the team lost. It is why there could be no rest until Newcastle were officially – mathematically – confirmed as a Premier League team, relevance restored, rebuilding job begun.

At Benitez's insistence, glory might have been shared out equally among every single member of staff at Newcastle. But promotion was for the people. His people.

1. End Of The Road

How Newcastle United Turned To Rafa Benitez

"We don't demand a team that wins.
We demand a team that tries"

Newcastle United fans' banner, circa 2015

IT was a slate grey Saturday afternoon in March when the reckoning that had been stalking Newcastle United for three years finally arrived.

St James' Park, in the dying days of a Tyneside winter. It was gloomy enough to require the floodlights to be switched on, shortly after the home side had kicked off against Bournemouth in a game billed as the most important of their ignoble 2015/16 season. As it turned out, the ominous skies had a point.

If it is possible for a crowd of 52,000 people to create an atmosphere of apathy, Newcastle United had somehow managed to do it for the seven months before Bournemouth's visit. They conspired to lose 17 of their 29 matches before the clocks went forward but the mood was one of resignation rather than rebellion.

"We are moving in the right direction," manager Steve McClaren had insisted when the two sides met earlier in the season. Newcastle had won 1-0 at Dean Court, facing down a South Coast storm and an onslaught from the home side to prevail.

But the progress that McClaren had spoken of never came. While others – newly-promoted Bournemouth among their number – had grown as the weeks went by, United's revival felt positively glacial. McClaren's arrested development was to be exposed on a day when the roof came in on Newcastle's house of straw.

Appropriately, it was an own goal that pushed the club closer to crisis point. Twenty minutes were on the clock when Bournemouth's Max Gradel, who began his football career playing for Lewisham College, darted into space on Newcastle's right flank and delivered a cross laced with menace into their penalty box. Steven Taylor, one of McClaren's unquestioningly loyal foot soldiers, stuck out a leg and diverted the ball past goalkeeper Rob Elliot. Whatever unity there had been between stands and an underperforming squad dissipated. The howls of disgust from the stands diminished McClaren's authority even further.

On the right of midfield, one player in Bournemouth pink stood out. The industrious winger Matt Ritchie was everything the Newcastle team were not: bright, inventive, incessant.

Back when he was a teenager trying to break into the first team at Dagenham & Redbridge he'd spoken to his future father-in-law John – a Newcastle supporter – about the prospect of playing in front of a full house at St James' Park. If those in black and white struggled to find motivation that day, Ritchie certainly did not. In the 70th minute, his persistence paid off. He fed Lewis Grabban and called for the ball back instantly. A wonderfully weighted first-time pass dissected Newcastle's defence and teed up striker Joshua King, whose shot was emphatic. At 2-0 there was no coming back for the home side.

McClaren stood impassively, a few feet from the touchline, soaking up the jeers of the supporters. At some modern football stadiums, the dug-outs have been deliberately moved a few yards from the supporters to prevent interaction but at St James' Park, they jut into the Milburn Stand and are surrounded by season-ticket holders. Unfortunately for McClaren photographers know this makes for the perfect picture. The home supporters had shown remarkable tolerance during his teething period but the portrait of the day depicted snarling fans letting McClaren know what they thought of a pathetic performance. His shoulders hunched in his over-sized black Puma jacket, McClaren cut a bereft figure.

The dressing room afterwards was funereal. The silence was broken by what seemed to be a primal scream from the rabble-rousing Taylor, the club's longest-serving outfield player. His was one of the only voices raised in anger. A few words of admonishment came from McClaren and Paul Simpson, his assistant, a decent man who shared the frustration of his friend at a performance that did not match the talent at his disposal. Those words were not delivered with any real venom, as if even those in charge were beginning to suspect the game was up.

The majority – including those signed from the Netherlands, Belgium and France in a four-week summer recruitment drive that was supposed to recalibrate Newcastle as a young, vibrant, attack-minded force – sat with heads bowed, silent. A matter-of-fact statement released before the match on behalf of the players, which many knew nothing about, insisted they still had confidence in McClaren but it did not reflect the eerily flat mood that hung over that room. Something had gone seriously wrong.

Later, in the bowels of the stadium as the supporters dispersed into the bars, restaurants and Metros, McClaren shuffled into the stadium's cavernous media room and attempted to conjure up a defiant response.

"This is the most frustrating team I've ever had," he said. "I still think this can be a great club but it needs things doing to it." The implication of that statement was clear. McClaren may have been the fall guy, but this was not solely his mess. He was bargaining for time and patience.

But in the boardroom they saw the numbers. Newcastle were 19th, a point off rivals Sunderland with 10 matches to play and a game in hand – against reigning champions Manchester City. Relegation would see £40m wiped off the club's revenue stream in an instant. The careful but controversial project to make the club self-sustaining was in peril. Having turned away from the nuclear option of changing manager twice before, they had run out of options. There was nowhere else for Newcastle to go.

****

McCLAREN was required to own the failure that day but he was not the architect of the problems that had turned Newcastle into a club that was not fit for Premier League purpose.

A bit of context is required to McClaren's last act. The team that plunged the knife into the Newcastle manager's fragile team that day were managed by the bright rising star of British management, Eddie Howe, who had led them on a remarkable journey through the uplands of English football's lower leagues. Newcastle had gone backwards while their combination of astute management on and off the pitch had seen them take great strides to catch up with the sport's more illustrious names. In 2012, Bournemouth had finished 11th in League One – a frustrating return for a team that had reached the division's play-offs in the previous year. Howe was at Burnley then but returned to Bournemouth, citing home sickness – and his comeback saw the Cherries promoted to the Championship in his first season back.

In the same season that Bournemouth were toiling to finish mid-table in the third tier, Newcastle ended up fifth in the Premier League – an achievement that earned Alan Pardew the LMA Manager of the Year award.

In the chairman's suite at St James' Park that May, Pardew threw a party for staff and correspondents who had covered a thoroughly unexpected success story. Sports Direct founder Mike Ashley – the club's controversial owner – had demanded changes to the way the club operated and his managing director, Derek Llambias, had ruthlessly implemented them. The pair of them couldn't understand the way the sport in England worked – the money wasted, the inefficiency of listening to supposed 'football men' and backing their judgement to the tune of millions of pounds. Too often those hunches proved expensive, unscientific mistakes. All around them they saw backs being scratched, friends looking after friends. Ashley had made his billions in sportswear before brokering the takeover of Newcastle and had been in sop to emotion when he brought Kevin Keegan back to St James' Park within 12 months of taking over in 2008. It was a nod to a golden era that caught the imagination beyond the club's traditional stronghold in the North East. But it did not work.

Ashley had trusted a cadre of confidantes with no respect for the club's traditions to work with Keegan but the tension made it unworkable. An early decision to give Dennis Wise an over-arching role in charge of football operations was incredible. Keegan had transformed Newcastle twice, winning over hearts and minds as a player and then once-in-a-lifetime manager but the third coming was shoddily handled by Ashley's men. Keegan would eventually win a tribunal against the club for constructive dismissal, awarded £2m in a judgement that was to have profound and lasting consequences. The fall-out changed the course of the club's history.

Keegan, rightfully a hero on Tyneside, became a vocal and persistent critic. Mistrust festered between owner and the club's supporters – Ashley put the club on the market and then hastily withdrew it, claiming no serious offers. Relegation followed, trust was broken and a more confrontational and unflinching path was embarked upon. Ashley felt that football's lores were pointless and needed to be broken up. In former casino manager Llambias, he found the perfect ally.

One player's agent remembers the procession of representatives to meetings at St James' Park in the summer of 2011 that preceded United's fifth-placed season as like "blood letting". Kevin Nolan – a man described by club stalwart Steve Harper as one of the best captains in Newcastle's history – was expecting negotiations over a new contract in recognition of his service. He was low-balled in talks, expected to sign a structured deal that would depend on games played. It was the sort of contract offer that a young player with something to prove would be presented with – not one that a club captain with Mark Curtis, one of the most powerful agents, representing him would accept. Newcastle were in no mood to compromise and over the English Channel, in French Flanders, they knew why.

Midfielder Yohan Cabaye had been the star of Lille's Ligue 1-winning side but the time had arrived for a new challenge. While Tyneside debated Nolan's new contract or how the club was going to replace Andy Carroll – sold for £35m to Liverpool in an incredible deal on the final day of the January transfer deadline, Newcastle's chief scout, Graham Carr, was in a taxi on his way to Stade Pierre-Mauroy to watch the match.

"The stamps on the passport are what help you to spot a player. Watch them, see them time and again but also talk to people. You can learn a lot from talking to the taxi drivers, the cafe owners," Carr reflected. He liked Cabaye from the moment he first saw him. There was an elegance about his passing range but he had an edge to his game, too. Carr believed he would settle quickly into the blood and thunder of the Premier League.

Negotiating transfers was like a game of poker to Llambias. Stack the decks in your favour and when you have a strong hand, the other side will either fold or take a gamble which backfires. With Cabaye, Newcastle's hand was strengthened by Carr pressing the flesh in France, speaking to the right middle men and the club selling itself ruthlessly to ambitious agents in mainland Europe. Newcastle knew of a clause in his contract that enabled them to get him for a knockdown £4m. Cabaye was told of plans to use the £35m banked from Carroll's sale to create a vibrant side of young, ambitious players that would get "bums off seats" at St James' Park. Standing against Newcastle was the tendency for overseas players to prefer to play in London or Manchester. To counter that, it was mentioned that playing in the Premier League was a platform to the world's biggest clubs. Newcastle wanted to get there themselves, of course, but the business logic was fairly ruthless. Play well enough and outgrow the club and as long as the deal's right, Newcastle will sell and re-invest in the next Cabaye.

Back home in Newcastle, there was a conflicted feel about proceedings. Nolan was offered a much better deal by West Ham United that he took – prompting Joey Barton, new to social media, to take aim at Newcastle over Twitter. 'Feel sick,' he wrote. A calamitous pre-season tour of America followed. Left-back Jose Enrique spoke out and was sold. Barton followed soon after, released on a free after a bust-up with Pardew. In came Demba Ba, another contacts job, signed for no fee but in an expensive deal amid a furious struggle between competing agents. Sylvain Marveaux, wanted by Liverpool but with a questionable fitness record, was another cheap import.

Tyneside held its breath for the season that followed but dire predictions of struggle were confounded. The Geordie 'moneyball' upset the apple cart – Newcastle's formula had them competing with teams that had supposedly greater resources. Sharp negotiating, good contacts, subverting some of football's tired dictats: Newcastle were on the up again. They narrowly missed out on the Champions League that season but the addition of another shrewd signing – Papiss Cisse – added to Carr's collection of rough diamonds that also included robust midfielder Cheick Tiote and the mercurial Hatem Ben Arfa, a rare talent flourishing among supporters who appreciated his flawed genius.

Over the course of a season, perceptions of Newcastle shifted. Ashley had been labelled as the poster boy for the worst kind of owner in the aftermath of Newcastle's 2009 relegation but now his ownership was hailed as visionary in some quarters. In Newcastle there remained plenty of suspicion towards the owner but nationally, there was a scramble to find out more. The requests for interviews with the top brass were so plentiful that they got fed up and eventually stopped granting them. Llambias seemed to like sycophancy less than he did criticism.

Still, there was cause to celebrate in May 2011, as anyone inside the chairman's suite for the post-season gathering would attest. Pardew was on his second glass of wine at that post-season celebration when the text informing him he was the Barclays Premier League Manager of the Year arrived. He did not expect it. "I didn't think I was well liked enough to win it," he candidly admitted to the reporters present.

But it was a deserved accolade: he had managed the squad deftly. He knew he was replacing a popular predecessor in Chris Hughton and had handled it well to this point. Pardew toasted the announcement before hot-footing it across the city to the studios of BBC Radio Newcastle for a listener phone-in. Over the airwaves he compared Ba and Cisse to Lady Gaga and Madonna, and spoke about exciting times to follow.

Newcastle's success that season was because they thought differently. Innovation came in their solution to the problem of replacing two big players – Carroll and Nolan – with something completely, utterly different. Cabaye was no Nolan and Ba was no Carroll. The critics said they were cheaper but it wasn't just the bottom line that was improved by their purchases.

The appointment of Fabricio Coloccini as captain was different, too. Newcastle wanted to be cosmopolitan. Every day at training that season, chef Liz Hornsby took on the cuisine of a nationality in the dressing room and the players were asked to liaise on the menu. Everyone was forced to dine together, not in cliques based around languages or passports.

The most important thing was that Newcastle were pitch perfect when it came to recruitment. The club's power brokers had sat down to talk about the approach long before Carr began making those trips to the north of France. They did not want to be the last home of established internationals seeking a final pay day at a club that had been seen in agent circles as easy money. Pulling together a sales pitch to signings, Newcastle's hierarchy listed their financial might in comparison to around 14 out of 20 teams in the Premier League in the column labelled strengths. They could pay more in wages and afford the transfer fees that would be beyond rivals like Stoke City, Aston Villa and Sunderland. Being first off the mark for players that the top four or five did not see as accomplished enough for their squads was to be the priority. Cisse, Ba, Tiote and Ben Arfa were perfect deals. Arsene Wenger, surveying the success of Cabaye, summoned his Arsenal scouting team and asked them why they had not spotted his potential and known about his price tag. He wasn't the only one surprised by Newcastle's success.

But it was to prove hideously short-lived. The alchemy was fleeting. Newcastle had profited from other clubs' failings to adapt, but they themselves were caught unaware by a series of developments that re-arranged the order in the Premier League.

First, they failed to address the shift in mood in the dressing room. Players wanted improved contracts and others, whose heads were turned by interest elsewhere, sought reassurances that further spending would match their own ambitions to be top six year in, year out. Newcastle did not listen. Resentment grew.

Cabaye walked out on the team before the first game of the season at Manchester City when he was refused permission to talk to Arsenal, and Coloccini stood up for him in a dressing room meeting that followed. It was an ominous precedent, that most of the squad sympathised with the ambitious player rather than the club. Sure enough, ruthlessly ambitious Ba left at the first opportunity. It was a process of curdling team spirit that was to last four years.

Secondly, Newcastle missed the redistribution of financial power in the Premier League that eventually caused the seismic shock of Leicester's incredible title win. Tyneside's financial advantage was wiped out in a stroke by a £3b Premier League TV deal struck with Sky and BT that saw money distributed across the division, to clubs like Stoke City, the Foxes and even previous yo-yo clubs like Crystal Palace. Suddenly, anyone could play Newcastle's game – and many did it better than them. The emergence of Dmitri Payet and Riyad Mahrez, both players from Ligue 1 who took the Premier League by storm, cut deep at Newcastle. That they starred in the claret of West Ham and the blue of Leicester against Newcastle in the 2015/16 season further emphasised how tired their formula had become.

Thirdly, having negotiated skilfully with Cabaye, Tiote and company they became obsessed with the perfect transfer deal and missed opportunities in the transfer market. In fairness, they were difficult deals. United went in low on striker Alexandre Lacazette of Lyon and did not manage to sign him. A private jet was chartered to watch Pierre-Emerick Aubameyang play for Saint-Etienne but the deal proved beyond Newcastle. Both players developed into two of Europe's most coveted players.

Frustration and tension built and clear thinking became muddled. The appointment of Joe Kinnear as director of football in 2013 ended any talk of Newcastle's model being a beacon for others. His swearing interview with TalkSPORT a few days after Ashley asked him to take on the role – in which he mispronounced Cabaye's name as 'Kebab' among other indignities – ushered in a new era of calamity.

****

TWO fraught years passed but it was against this backdrop that McClaren emerged, blinking, into the summer sun at Newcastle's Benton training base in 2015.

By now Llambias was gone, having resigned after Kinnear's appointment made his position – in his view – untenable. He was replaced by Lee Charnley, who had climbed the ranks at Newcastle from club secretary to managing director.

Born in Lancashire but having worked at Newcastle for more than a decade, Charnley's remit was to end the underachievement. So he thought differently, constructing a management model that did without the "old-fashioned manager", as he put it. The new man would be a "head coach", responsible for football affairs with the caveat that transfers and recruitment would be shared with Carr, promoted to the board, and the MD himself.

Charnley's ultimate aim was to make Newcastle more consistent and robust – not beholden to the wild swings in mood that have become part and parcel of modern Premier League life, especially at a one-city club like his.

In my first meeting with him – an interview that remains the only one he's ever granted – in his airy office overlooking the bustling Newcastle city centre he held his hand at eye level and said that he wanted United to plot a consistent and constructive path through the middle, when others were getting either carried away with their success or contemplating the short-term shock to the system of changing management or personnel. It may not have been popular but there was a sort of sense to it.

Charnley made few friends among the supporters by making public the club's philosophy at the time to be the best it could be "pound-for-pound". It was meant to be aspirational – punching above where it should be in terms of revenue and budget – but it was cold and corporate. It reflected a hierarchy that had lost touch with the essence of the club.

The other mistake Newcastle made was believing McClaren looked like perfect "head coach" material. He was a decent coach but his management CV was sketchy, and his greatest attraction also proved to be his Achilles heel: he was prepared to accept every limitation that came with the role.

It was another jab in the face for traditionalists who felt a manager should have all-encompassing power. It also sketched out a picture of the type of person Newcastle wanted: someone prepared to work within what Charnley characterised as a "triangular management structure". Cynics presciently predicted that a big personality with a CV to match would not be interested.

McClaren most certainly was and after a protracted pursuit, he was finally named Newcastle manager on June 10. By then, almost all of the preparatory work had been done on signings. And his credibility suffered when he allowed the club to dictate the terms of his introductory press conference – limiting it to one publication who had a commercial arrangement with owner Ashley's Sports Direct. It was the first time ever that *The Chronicle* – the influential local newspaper – was not present at a managerial announcement. Intrepid journalists stood outside the stadium looking for answers but were not allowed in. The following day's headlines made for painful reading for McClaren.

The air of farce clung to him, despite his efforts to modernise Newcastle's style of play. He hammered home the importance of possession to his players. Jack Colback, a holding midfielder signed from Sunderland, said that the emphasis in training was on being in control of the ball. McClaren, inspired by young coach Ian Cathro, told his players they needed to have control of a passage of play before trying to move on to the next phase. What that meant in practice was that after six passes he would deem Newcastle to be in control of the ball. The idea was to start to dominate games – an antidote to the way they had played under Alan Pardew and John Carver, when the club had gone more direct.

McClaren had played this way during stints in Germany and the Netherlands but he was out of step with the trend of that season. It was a year when Leicester ripped up the rule book by winning the league while regularly recording less than 50 per cent of possession – something graphically illustrated at St James' Park when they tore Newcastle apart in a 3-0 thrashing in November.

McClaren believed in neuro-linguistic programming, where certain language patterns can influence the perception of the audience. He started to use buzz words, repeating them incessantly. In one press conference in December, he repeated the word "confidence" 32 times. Other words including "feisty" and the phrases "confidence is fragile" and "change is painful". They were bizarre interludes in a desperate season.

McClaren was close to the sack twice, pulling back from the brink by leading Newcastle to a 2-0 win over Liverpool in December. The second time, after a 5-1 defeat to Chelsea in February, Charnley took some soundings from the dressing room. There were signs McClaren was losing them – in an interview after the Stamford Bridge debacle Georginio Wijnaldum hinted that he felt he was being scapegoated for the poor performance – but enough people stood up for him. Charnley erred on the side of caution and McClaren kept his job, taking the team to La Manga for a supposedly restorative training break during a free weekend.

But the tensions remained and spilled over in the press conference before the fateful Bournemouth game as he called out a reporter over a story, claiming he was just one defeat from the sack. He was met with a fierce rebuttal from the journalist in scenes that did little to restore his authority in a dressing room that sniggered at the footage. A statement purporting to be from the players was released in the run-up to kick-off claiming they were still behind McClaren, but some disowned it privately. The 3-1 defeat that followed showed what they thought of it.

Given Charnley's reticence to sack managers, McClaren's exit came sooner than many expected but felt inevitable. When he was eventually put out of his misery, six days after the Bournemouth game and with the identity of his successor an open secret, the call eventually came from Charnley. He was thanked. It was cordial. A generous compensation package made it a softer landing.

"I went in with my eyes open and I knew the situation I was getting myself into, but the mistake I made was that I compromised too much. You have to go in, lead and manage. I compromised, especially early on, instead of saying, 'We need this, we need that'," he admitted afterwards.

Newcastle desperately needed change, but it was not just the manager. Deep-rooted problems lay in wait for the next man to try to revive Newcastle – issues that McClaren did not have the force of personality, or weight of authority to change. Newcastle's approach felt jaded and tired. The support was totally disenchanted and the dressing room felt that antipathy. Losing had seeped into the black and white bone marrow. McClaren, like Pardew and his successor, John Carver, identified the dressing room as a problem that needed to be fixed. He felt there was a desperate need for more character and leadership in a team that surrendered too readily in the face of adversity.

He went to the board with the names of players who were available for nothing and could bring that. One of them was Nolan. The other was Barton. He was told he had more chance of signing the Pope to play in a Newcastle shirt.

2. Luring Rafa

Why He Chose Newcastle United

"On our first date, he explained what 4-4-2 was. He finds it hard to stay away from the game"

Montse Benitez

FRANCISCO DE MIGUEL MORENO had just got in from a long afternoon bike ride when his mobile phone buzzed.

The man Rafa Benitez knows as 'Paco' is a bundle of energy: a live wire former student athlete who doubled up in the 1,500m and 10,000m, and whose times took him to the brink of the Spanish national athletics squad when he was younger. In his professional life, he's criss-crossed the globe, building a reputation as a coach and a thinker at a kaleidoscope of clubs as varied as West Brom, Getafe, Atletico Madrid and, most recently, their bigger footballing brother, Real Madrid.

An assistant coach with responsibility for overseeing the medical department, he had followed Benitez through the door of some of Europe's biggest clubs. His natural home was the training pitch, not behind the handlebars of a mountain bike.

The break was fine. Who wouldn't welcome the chance to breathe the mountain air in early spring? But being out of a job didn't suit him. The phone call was a welcome one.

The voice on the other end of the phone was instantly recognisable. There were a few short pleasantries before the two men got down to the business at hand. "Paco," he said. "What do you think of Newcastle? It is an option."

It was the first week of March. Football men know these as the season's moving months, when clubs fight for titles, relevance or – as in Newcastle United's case – survival. It wasn't really like Benitez to be watching from the sides, pen in hand, analysing while clubs tried to find solutions in the final months of the season. He'd done a punditry stint with BT Sport, adding expertise to their Champions League coverage and announcing his preference to return to the Premier League almost as soon as he lost his job with Real Madrid.

But the phone calls he wanted hadn't come until the vacancy at Newcastle, 19th in the Premier League and in real danger of dropping into the Championship. It was not the Bernabeu but when communication came from the North East, he was interested. He wanted to know if his friends felt the same. Moreno did not need to think about it.

"If we want to go back to England, this is a very good choice," 'Paco' said. The pair discussed the club's history, how its culture was so similar to Liverpool, where Benitez had announced his arrival to an English audience a decade before. They felt the job was difficult but not impossible.

"I was pushing for Newcastle from the start. Personally, I was very keen on coming to the club," Moreno says, looking back at that phone call. "I said that we have to see what happens but we have to have confidence in our work. Maybe, looking back, we didn't have all of the information at that point but we were confident that we could stay in the Premier League. And if I was to go back and offer advice with the knowledge I have of the club now, I'd say exactly the same thing."

Newcastle, he says, is a 'special' city. To work for its football club is a 'privilege' that he does not lose sight of.

Benitez said thanks and that he'd be in touch again soon.

***

LEE CHARNLEY will have to live with the criticism that he acted too late to remedy Newcastle's problems – issues, his detractors will claim, that had plenty to do with the way he had re-structured the club in the summer of 2015.

The alternative argument is that, at most of the stages of the season, when there was a compelling argument to sack McClaren and his coaching staff, there was no ready-made replacement ready to replace a head coach who pulled results out of the fire when Newcastle were giving serious thought to making a change.

The first signs of problems had come very early in that season at West Ham in September. Newcastle had aspired to over-achieve when they dreamt up a new way of recruiting and operating after their relegation and subsequent promotion in 2010, but the club had developed a soft underbelly that was exposed far too often by Premier League rivals. Under Pardew they found it difficult to come back from behind and developed a habit of losing heavily after conceding the first goal. Instilling more spirit in the group was going to be crucial to preventing more problems at Newcastle. McClaren had been briefed about it in detail when he took the job, but there was little to suggest it had been remedied that Monday night at Upton Park. Newcastle lost 2-0 after arriving at the ground late, their coach stuck in traffic and curtailing their pre-match warm-up. Mike Ashley was watching and was angry: observers said he sent the MD away with a "flea in his ear". But everyone was in agreement that it was too early, with six games gone, to do anything drastic.

Besides, Charnley's instinct was to show patience. Football's hiring-and-firing culture is expensive and short-term fixes do not always bring about the upturn in results that are intended. Even when they do – as they had done across the River Tyne at Sunderland – the lesson has not always been that changing managers creates a culture conducive to long-term success.

Charnley really, truly believed that, too. Newcastle had, incredibly, backed Pardew through fan walk-outs and protest because they were aspiring to the kind of stability that had helped Arsene Wenger and Sir Alex Ferguson to build dynasties at Arsenal and Manchester United. The only time Pardew's job was at risk was when he told Sky's *Goals on Sunday* programme – in a more candid moment – that the club's owner "didn't really understand football". That did not go down well. Pardew was given a formal warning but, even then, he survived.

The problem with the stability logic was that Newcastle were circling the drain by December and a more drastic course of action had to at least be contemplated. Any list of replacements would have made for pretty uninspiring reading: Nigel Pearson, perhaps, would have had some credibility after his work keeping Leicester up. But he had baggage and his record did not stand out. He was not considered a better manager than McClaren.

Garry Monk had built a good team at Swansea that had won plaudits playing passing football but the step up to take charge of Newcastle – a club that required as much off the field managing as it did on it – would have been a big one.

David Moyes? The Scot was the first choice for the Newcastle job when Sam Allardyce was sacked by Ashley in 2008 but he didn't want to leave his Everton project. Since then his CV had been tarnished by failures at Real Sociedad and Manchester United, where his reputation took a substantial battering.

Brendan Rodgers had done decent work at Liverpool before losing focus and his job when Jurgen Klopp – an instant upgrade – became available. How Newcastle fans had silently seethed at the ambition at Anfield when Klopp, the sort of charismatic, ambitious manager who might electrify their club, took over there. It felt like proof of their position in the Premier League pecking order. Although he had his advocates, there was little enthusiasm for Rodgers on the terraces. It would not have been a transformative appointment.

None of those names did much for Newcastle.

The preference was to stick with McClaren if he was able to start turning things around and, sure enough, two results in December changed everything. Newcastle bounced back from a dreadful 5-1 defeat at Crystal Palace to beat a lacklustre Liverpool 2-0 in their best home performance of the season, before going to Tottenham and securing a brilliant, injury-time win at a shell-shocked White Hart Lane. McClaren told people at the club that it was "clicking" and, with a decent January transfer window, they would move clear of relegation trouble in 2016. Charnley agreed and significant funds were released to buy winger Andros Townsend, midfielder Henri Saivet, Seydou Doumbia and England international Jonjo Shelvey – a player Newcastle were delighted to sign from relegation rivals Swansea City.

There was hope – but the storm had not passed. A brief uptick in form – wins over West Ham and West Brom temporarily lifted Newcastle out of the relegation zone – was arrested by the cold, hard reality of the club failing to address the bigger issues corroding its form.

Sure enough, by February the revival had been strangled by the same issues that had dogged Newcastle all season: a dressing room incapable of responding to setbacks, full of too many sullen senior professionals. It was unbalanced. Even some of those who were inside it felt it was toxic.

When Jamaal Lascelles was sent off at Everton in a 3-0 defeat the defender was caught on a pitchside mic saying, 'No-one gives a f***'. Battening down the hatches – a Newcastle tactic that had served them well during Pardew's brief tenure – felt increasingly like an approach that had run its course.

The clamour for a change reached fever pitch after a 5-1 defeat at Stamford Bridge. Newcastle, knocked out of the FA Cup, would have two weeks without a game and there would be a chance for a new man to stamp his authority on the club. It made sense, but when Charnley took soundings, there was not the discontent with McClaren that might have been imagined. He wanted to know whether the head coach had lost the players. The answer, surprisingly, was that they liked McClaren. They felt he could turn it around. A common theme was that the break would give the club a chance to get players back for the run-in. Two weeks would re-focus minds. The MD stepped back from the brink and agreed to pay for a sunshine break to the La Manga training facilities at which the head coach could salvage the situation.

But something had changed in the 90 days that separated the December crisis and the one staring Charnley in the face at the start of spring: Benitez.

Newcastle had a head coach but football is a claustrophobic world. There is a whole industry of intermediaries who ask the questions that clubs cannot officially pose and, after a few feelers were put out, word was delivered back to Tyneside that the Spaniard would be interested in a conversation if they decided to make a change.

Benitez, an obsessive with a razor-sharp eye for detail, needed to do background checks. His phone never stopped ringing. For Newcastle, it was much more straightforward. Fourteen months before Charnley and club ambassador Bob Moncur took a train out of Newcastle Central station to meet Benitez and his advisors, the MD had told the local newspaper, *The Chronicle*, that the days of an old-fashioned manager at Newcastle were over.

Now, in the club's hour of need, he was prepared to admit that battle had been lost. Benitez was polite but driven in initial meetings: his ambitions for the club struck everyone. He had watched and re-watched DVDs of Newcastle's games that season and was struck by the last of them, against Bournemouth. He made a point of saying that Newcastle would need to re-engage the fans for the final games of the season. He personally penned the opening line of the statement that announced his appointment. 'C'mon Toon Army. The club and I need your total involvement,' it read. It was a bit clumsy, but it felt authentic.

For McClaren, it was the longest of goodbyes. Newcastle's next match following the Bournemouth debacle was against top-of-the-table Leicester and had been moved to a Monday night for television, which meant the players started his final week with a day off. But with speculation surrounding his future running wild, he turned up dutifully on Tuesday, and then again on Wednesday and Thursday. Photographers on the perimeter of the training ground recorded his every move outside the club's Darsley Park offices and one image summed up that ignominious week. In it, the club's long-serving security guard, Graeme Crombie – 'Tash' to those who work there, on account of his facial hair – is patting McClaren on the back. But from the angle it's taken, it looks as though McClaren is being bundled into the back of a getaway car. The man in the picture might have wished he was but, to his credit, he continued to take training sessions while the rest of the world knew his fate was as good as sealed.

Charnley took more criticism. Pilloried for not acting, now he was criticised for not concluding the deal with Benitez's lawyers quickly enough. National columnists said it was another example of United's lack of dignity, stringing McClaren along. He retained a sort of gallows humour. "So, can you tell me what's going on then?" he laughed, when called in the middle of the furore.

On Thursday, it was still with the lawyers. Benitez had been warned to get everything in writing before signing up for the challenge, which explained the tortuous delay. By Friday, it was – finally – done. The first statement confirming McClaren's exit arrived not long before the one confirming Benitez – by now in a hotel in the North East and having been spotted near the stadium – had been appointed. It was a sad end for McClaren, whose own statement said that he had been privileged to work at a club that was the "embodiment of the city", although it was not without its perks. He had made just shy of £700,000 for his time at Newcastle and would be guaranteed another £1m if he did not find work quickly afterwards.

Perhaps Charnley, a relatively young MD in the world of football, would not admit it but the appointment of Benitez must have come as a blessed relief.

By the time Benitez was introduced as Newcastle's new manager, Charnley's stock had plummeted with the club's fans. A man who had a reputation as a straight shooter with agents – "He is good, an honest bloke, you know where you stand with him" one said – it had been a troubled spell at the top, balancing the club's ambitions with a need to run the club along owner Ashley's very strict parameters. The two things did not always seem compatible and it had proved a tough introduction to life at the top.

Although he had ridden a fans' boycott in 2014 and only reluctantly made the McClaren change, this decision felt like a final roll of the dice.

It was a popular one, though. It was the right one and if Charnley took the slings and arrows for previous failings, he deserved credit for taking this gamble. The surge of interest after Benitez was appointed gave *The Chronicle* one of its best-selling editions of the year. Fans could scarcely believe that after Pardew, John

Carver and McClaren, a man whose CV was the equal of any in world football would give Newcastle a second look. Even fewer had believed the club would have the ambition or desire to go for someone whose approach so clearly contradicted the 'triangle of power' management model that McClaren was hampered by.

It was a working day when Benitez arrived in a silver people carrier but word had seeped out, and a few fans on their lunch break assembled at St James' Park, smart phones out, recording. It was not the thousands who had turned up for Alan Shearer's unveiling in the days when Newcastle aspired to win titles and break world-record transfer fees, but the excitement was genuine. The mood of the city was lifted in an instant.

There is a myth that clings to Newcastle that the support has unrealistic aspirations that suffocate good managers and players. But take a trip to the city, walk up Monument to the statue of Charles Grey that peers down on the shoppers below and you'll find a different mood among match-going fans. There is a fervour but the only demand – as a banner displayed during the 2015/16 run-in made clear – is not for a team that has to wins, but a club that tries to win. A lucrative cottage nostalgia industry for the days when Kevin Keegan's teams entertained the country but did not quite win the Premier League title feels like proof of that.

More recently, the club's lack of ambition saw them admit that the FA Cup – a competition that is part of Newcastle's rich heritage, with three wins in the 1950s – was no longer a priority. They reneged on that a year later but it cut deep. Part of the excitement at Benitez's arrival stemmed from the fact that most of Newcastle's supporters were stunned that someone of his ability would look at them twice.

But Benitez had sniffed out something. His instinct was that Newcastle was a club whose natural constituency was the top eight of the Premier League and he felt the same yearning that he'd experienced when he arrived in Merseyside all those years before.

"They are both working-class cities. The people work hard. They love their football. We can smell football in Liverpool – you can smell it here," he said at his unveiling.

***

BENITEZ was appointed before lunchtime on Friday. A scheduled day off for the players. His first move was to ask for a text to be sent to all of the first-team squad requesting they attend a meeting that afternoon. They should be prepared to train. He wanted to be back on the pitch as soon as possible. Within 90 minutes of his appointment, he was.

The club, cannily, beamed the first bit of the training session on social media site Twitter, filming all of it live on the Periscope app. It was a smart move that won Benitez quick and easy credit among supporters.

"We knew we didn't have much time," he says, looking back at his decision to call a training session on that frenzied afternoon. "We knew we had to play against Leicester, who were at the top of the table, and we did not have too much time to prepare for such a tough game. We had to get our message across straight away. It was quite quick but we needed to do it."

At the training ground, staff that had felt on edge suddenly sensed that someone with real presence had walked into the building. He was joined by his loyal lieutenants 'Paco', Antonio Gomez – a former player who had become a coaching understudy and Claudio Pecchia, an ex-professional with Napoli and Juventus who also has a law degree. They are an intense group who could converse freely in three languages – but Benitez told them to talk exclusively in English to put everyone's minds at rest. For continuity Benitez retained Ian Cathro, a young Scottish coach who had worked in Portugal before joining Newcastle.

His first request was for a louder whistle. The second was for more footballs. He shook hands with everyone. It felt like Newcastle might have a chance.

"It was emotional. I knew that I was signing for a massive club, a big city with a massive support from the fans," he says, looking back at March 11.

"It was an important moment for me. To be back in the Premier League was special."

***

SO why did Benitez risk his reputation by signing up for a salvage job at a club written off, even by its own fans, as a basket case?

The advice he took before arriving at Newcastle's Benton training ground from Alan Shearer, Kenny Dalglish, Michael Owen and Peter Beardsley played its part. When his wife, Montse – whose knowledge of football is almost as razor-sharp as her husband's – asked him whether he really wanted to try and awaken one of English football's comatose sleeping giants, he seemed enthused by the scale of the challenge. She ran through a list of some of the big characters who had failed – Dalglish and Ruud Gullit being two of the biggest managerial talents to fall flat on their faces – but Benitez did not see the potential pitfalls.

For a start, it was back in England with his family. Offers to go to China or Turkey for more money than was on the table at Newcastle had arrived but weren't attractive. He wanted to spend more time with his two daughters. Newcastle is a three-and-a-half hour drive from the family home in Wirral, but it is closer than Naples or Madrid. The Premier League was where he'd most enjoyed his time and where he wanted to return.

More importantly, Benitez had done two months out of the game and was ready to return. Football management is his life: his honeymoon was spent in Milan, where he broke off from sightseeing to watch the first team train with a pen and pad. The last time Benitez had spent a prolonged period out of the game, he was spotted walking his dog in Caldy and asked to help out coaching the local school team.

"It was hilarious," Montse told the *Liverpool Echo* in 2015. "He stood on the sidelines and shouted at them as if they were First Division players, waving his arms about. He doesn't see football as work, it's his passion."

It was a million miles away from the superstars of Madrid, but that obsession was to take him to Tyneside.

3. Mission Impossible

Why Rafa Benitez Couldn't Keep Newcastle In The Premier League

"I think Newcastle has got into him a little bit in terms of the reaction of the fans. It's a bit like Newcastle can't believe they have got a coach who is at that level, who has managed Real Madrid, who's been managing Cristiano Ronaldo and wants to manage Newcastle"

Jamie Carragher, May 2016

RAFA BENITEZ had drawn up a list. Ten games, three columns. Before he had shaken hands on the Newcastle United salvage job, the obsessive details man had already done the mathematics.

It did not feel like mission impossible for Newcastle on the dreamy weekend that followed confirmation of regime change –

and a tentative new era – at St James' Park. Benitez's appointment had exhilarated a fanbase not used to unabashed positivity, and the mixture of disbelief and delight made for a potent cocktail. "I had not felt that way about my football club for a long time," Alex Hurst, now editor of the *True Faith* fanzine – a bellwether for Newcastle fan opinion – says. Hope had returned. It was an emotion many fans hadn't felt for years.

Benitez knew that tapping into that was going to be key. "In the matches, I think the fans can be our number 12," he had said with a smile at his unveiling. But there was more cold, hard logic at play over a long weekend at Newcastle's Benton training ground. Newcastle were 19th, level on points with Norwich City but two goals behind them. Sunderland – starting to pick up form under former Newcastle manager Sam Allardyce, a Benitez nemesis – were a point further on in the final safety spot. Bottom-of-the-league Aston Villa had 16 points and were dead and buried. Swansea City and Crystal Palace were both on 33, nine points ahead of Newcastle but having played a game more than the Magpies. Newcastle had both to play but Benitez did not feel either could realistically be caught.

So he gathered the team and told them that their job was clear: to win the three-team mini-league that they currently sat bottom of. He felt the first XI had talent but he acknowledged that the squad had little balance. He was surprised that there was no fit left-footed player at the club when he arrived. Contingency planning had gone out of the window. "I had my eyes open but we had problems," he acknowledges.

Benitez arrived in Newcastle prepared to play to the strengths of the squad. There were few goals in the team and they conceded too easily but, with an emphasis on improved concentration and a more robust system, he felt they could begin to chisel out points. A mythical 'new manager bounce' is often talked about in football, when a fresh voice and different direction brings a surge in form. For Benitez, the importance was not to over-complicate things. He didn't want to become over-burdened by what had gone before or the problems – political, personality – that still festered. He wanted the players to concentrate more. The first three days before Leicester were about delivering clear, concise instructions to the players about what was expected of them. That meant longer hours on the training ground but there was a purpose to it all. Imposing a new philosophy would have to wait.

An initial glance at the injury list confirmed the club's best defender – captain and long-serving centre-back Fabricio Coloccini – and their best defensive midfielder, Cheick Tiote, would not be available for his first game against the division's surprise leaders, Leicester City, at the King Power Stadium. Benitez wanted to construct a more formidable defensive unit at St James' Park and those two players could have been crucial. Never mind. He would have to be more flexible. He asked Coloccini to come to training sessions to offer his experience. He spoke to him and leant on the captain's advice, and his unvarnished opinions on where things were going wrong.

"When we came, we had 12 or 13 players injured at the same time," Benitez says, over a year on from that first training session. "We were unlucky. The timing was not good and the first game was against the team at the top of the Premier League with little time to prepare. We couldn't choose the fixture list so my attitude was, 'Just get on with it'."

Benitez noticed other things: the training ground felt dark. There was not enough natural light in the building. Some of the staff he met were a bit too quiet, almost subdued. Little things, but indicative of a club with deeper problems that needed more than just cosmetic changes to address their poor form.

Other things: there were too many younger players far from the first team milling around the club's Benton training base. They were sent back to the Academy headquarters down the road. "We needed focus," Benitez reasoned. These were smaller issues to wrestle with. But the lack of a left-back was a real problem.

"The first problem was that we did not have a left full-back. For our first games we had to play Vurnon Anita at left-back – a right-footed midfielder. Then it was Jack Colback, another midfielder. Then Anita again," he says.

"After three games we had Paul Dummett and we were really pleased. A left-footer! We have a left-footer who can play parallel to the line, rather than someone who will pull the ball in on his right foot. Those things were difficult in the beginning."

English football lore usually dictates that when you hit 40 points, survival is assured. Only one team in two decades had gone down with that total – West Ham in 2003.

History offered Benitez clues about the total required. In the previous five seasons, 37 points would have been enough – just. So 38 should do it and, looking at the fixtures the other teams had, 39 points would be a nice insurance policy. That would put it beyond doubt. By those calculations Newcastle probably needed 14 points from the final 10 games. Do-able, everyone agreed.

Wins? Newcastle had Sunderland, Norwich and Aston Villa. Two of them had to yield the full three points. Crystal Palace and Swansea – both at St James' Park – were the other fixtures that looked winnable.

Those were the positives. Newcastle also had five of the top eight left to play: the leaders, on their own patch, and games at home to Spurs and Manchester City. That latter one did not have a date next to it on account of the Citizens' extended adventures in the Champions League. They were flying high but had weaknesses. Benitez wanted a new date to be sorted out straight away. Timing could be of the essence.

Benitez hadn't really thought about the fact that the first home game – a Tyne-Wear derby – would bring him back into contact with Allardyce, a former Newcastle manager who had written in his autobiography that Liverpool's 2005 Champions League success had little to do with him.

Allardyce felt like the perfect fit for Sunderland, a club locked in a perennial relegation battle that too often seemed only to respond in the adversity that came with a desperate battle for survival. He was unfashionable, abrasive, arrogant and unapologetic. He had cajoled money out of the club's owner, Ellis Short, signing central defender Lamine Kone from Lorient in a deal that had proved tortuous to conclude.

His agent was prevented from entering the Academy of Light at one point, leaving Kone and his adviser holed up in the Hilton Hotel in Newcastle. A call was made to Newcastle to enquire if they wanted him instead. The offer was declined. Kone eventually signed for Sunderland and had proved an instant hit, exactly the sort of physical presence the club needed at the back.

Allardyce had liked Steve McClaren, partly because he was taking Newcastle down. Benitez, for all Allardyce found him cold and alien, provided Sunderland with something to worry about. Not that Allardyce seemed unduly concerned by his newest North East managerial colleague.

'Of course he can say he won the Champions League with Liverpool, which is something I never did. But it was nowt to do with him,' Allardyce had written about Benitez in his book, *Big Sam.* 'I don't blame Benitez for claiming credit but, as managers, we know the truth. It's like when you make a substitution in desperation and it comes off. You get all the credit for your tactical brilliance when it's often just luck.'

Benitez responded in kind, questioning Allardyce's own CV. "He has a book to sell – his opinion is of no value," he told a Spanish radio station.

On Wearside, Allardyce cracked a smile when he was asked the inevitable question after Benitez's appointment. The pair's enmity had been deep-rooted at one point, Benitez reasoning – quite rightly – that his closeness to Sir Alex Ferguson made him more foe than friend. But the feud had run out of fuel by the point the pair turned up in the North East.

"There is nothing Rafa can say or do that is going to rattle me," Allardyce said. Benitez agreed. He had far bigger problems to wrestle with.

***

ALMOST two decades to the day before Newcastle pitched up in the East Midlands on a Monday in mid-March, Kevin Keegan's 'Entertainers' were beginning to unravel.

The year 1996 still impacts on the football club and, some would argue, the city of Newcastle. A 12-point lead at the top of the Premier League had been earned by a buccaneering spirit that had lifted Keegan's side into the public consciousness. They looked unstoppable in early February but Manchester United's belligerence proved a thorn in their side.

Manchester United were in town on March 4, 1996. A mere four points separated the two teams. Victory might have quelled the red rising. Avoiding defeat would have been enough. But Newcastle's performance reflected the mood of the city. Eric Cantona had the craft to beat the home side's furious efforts, which were brilliantly repelled by Peter Schmeichel. *The Chronicle's* match report read: 'The silence was deafening as thousands of Geordies left their field of dreams with hunched shoulders and nostrils heavy with the scent of defeat.

'A Premier League lead, once 12 points with a game in hand, is now down to a solitary point and the funeral parade outside of St James' Park reflected the mood of an area.'

Claudio Ranieri's Foxes did not play like Keegan's side. While there was a wonderful attacking anarchy to the Newcastle of 1996 – summed up as a belief that they could always score one goal more than their opposition – Leicester of 2016 were more subversive. There was a high-press, punk rock fury about their counter-attacking play. They were like nothing the Premier League had seen before.

The country had been electrified by their story but, for many on Tyneside, the memories of their only Premier League title charge remained too raw to celebrate this underdog story. Time has softened some of the pain in Newcastle, but that failure is now in the club's DNA. Bad management, poor judgement and the wrong players might have contributed to the club's under-achievement since then, but 1996 has played its part, too. The wistful supporters often wonder about the transformative impact winning that title might have had on Newcastle without realising it did change the club forever.

It still weighs heavily, sitting silently on the shoulders of anyone who tries to end that long, tortuous spell without lifting a major trophy. Now it was the turn of Leicester to apply some fresh salt to the wounds.

That they seemed free of the sort of tension that suffocated Newcastle's class of 1996 summed up their most unlikely of triumphs. Benitez had spent three good days on the training ground but he had to pick Colback, a midfielder, at left-back. He was an ever-present presence on the touchline, cajoling the defence into the right positions, barking orders from the sides. Waving his hands like he had on the touchline at that Wirral middle school. It felt good to be back – even if the result did Newcastle no favours.

Benitez's side had looked better and more organised but were undone by a 25th-minute overhead kick from Shinji Okazaki. It was the sort of goal Newcastle had been conceding all season, a moment of magic that was too easily conjured from defensive chaos. Afterwards, when he viewed the DVD, the Spaniard grew increasingly frustrated. "The ball bounced too much in our box," he reflected.

Leicester went five points clear that night. They looked nerveless, revelling in the pressure of the title fight. The bookies' 5,000-1 shot were proving what could be done if momentum took hold. They were not going to choke.

Despite the result, the industry and intensity had pleased Benitez. There was at least no sign of the surrender that had undermined McClaren.

***

BENITEZ sat back in his training ground office and explained the reason for the intensity of his work.

The Spaniard and his team arrive for work at 7am every day. Rarely a moment goes by when there isn't a hum of noise from one of the desks that form a circle in the coaches' room.

"The players will follow you if everything is right and they see the message is right," he says – explaining why hitting the ground running is so important to him.

"The players understand football, too. If you explain it right and say, 'You have to do this because this will happen', and then it does, they will keep following you. But if you say, 'Play long balls, we will be fine', and then you lose, they will not follow you.

"People talk about the reputation of the manager. Maybe he is an ex-player with a big reputation. But after two or three months the name doesn't matter. They only judge you on what is happening. And they will only follow you if the message is right."

Warming to the theme, he continued. "You can be a big name but if the message is wrong, you have problems. Which is why it doesn't matter what you have done – you have to keep working hard and getting it right."

Benitez's message was reinforced day after day but he kept unearthing problems. Papiss Cisse, the club's best hope for goals, was injured when Benitez took the job and looked rusty when he came back. Benitez shared the opinion of his predecessor that Seydou Doumbia, the panic buy striker signed to provide back-up to him, did not look good enough to play Premier League football. Alan Shearer – that great Newcastle goalscorer – had spoken of a corrosive losing mentality at the club and, at one point, in the ill-fated 2015/16 campaign, the win ratio across all of the clubs' representative teams dipped below 15 per cent for the season. The Academy team had been knocked out of the FA Youth Cup by AFC Wimbledon.

The views of rival coaches were eye-opening. After Newcastle were thrashed 5-1 at Crystal Palace, Eagles coach John Salako delivered the most damning of verdicts. "What we said in the dressing room was: 'Listen, let's not let this side get up. Knock the spirit out of them and then they will go.'

"Newcastle didn't earn the right to win the game. They let us walk all over them."

Benitez saw that, too, but gradually he managed to imbue a spirit in them at last. The next game was billed as the biggest of the season – a derby game against Sunderland. Newcastle were second best for much of the match, behind for more than half an hour to Jermain Defoe's goal.

St James' Park responded: momentum was, for the first time, with the home side. Aleksandar Mitrovic equalised with seven minutes to go and the noise became cacophonous – but they couldn't find the winner. A point wasn't really enough.

Two more defeats were more damaging. Against Norwich, Newcastle self-destructed. They coped with a yellow whirlwind at Carrow Road and Mitrovic seemed to have rescued a point at 2-2 with an 86th-minute penalty. Martin Olsson's goal in the third minute of stoppage-time was a sucker punch.

Then at Southampton, frustrations that Benitez had kept under the surface erupted. Newcastle were 3-0 down after 45 minutes and Daryl Janmaat punched a wall in frustration, fracturing a bone in his hand. Newcastle's soft underbelly was exposed on the south coast and Benitez – though furious – stood back and let Lascelles round on his fellow professionals in the dressing room afterwards, with accusations being flung back and forth.

Astonishingly, it bled out of the dressing room. "We need players who care," Lascelles said afterwards.

"We had Steve McClaren, who is a great manager, and now we've got Rafa Benitez, who is a great manager so it's clearly not that. It's the players and we have to take full responsibility. It's ourselves who need to change it and not the manager."

Lascelles, on at half-time at Southampton, started the following match. Others returned from the injury table and those that remained spent the week listening to the same messages. Something clicked: Sunderland won at Norwich in a result which was a double-edged sword for Newcastle. The victory was fantastic for the Black Cats but also dragged Norwich back into it, and gave Newcastle a glimmer of hope. But lose to Swansea and they'd be gone: they won 3-0. Then they took a point from Manchester City with their most Benitez performance of his spell so far: a display hewn with intelligence and counter-attacking poise. They fought back from two behind at Anfield on a day when all four corners of the ground sung Benitez's name. He was getting a taste for it and his team started to reflect the man: smart, compact, occasionally difficult but demanding of respect.

Pardew's return with Palace brought another three points and a 1-0 victory. Belief was returning. Newcastle were out of the bottom three at last on 33 points – two wins shy of the 39 that they believed would deliver top-flight survival. There were two games to play, the first of which was against an Aston Villa side that were already relegated.

However, what Benitez's mathematics had not accounted for was a Sunderland side that had been transformed by Allardyce. Their win at Norwich was backed up with a good point against

Arsenal at the Stadium of Light and a draw at Stoke. They had Chelsea, Everton and Watford to play, though.

Newcastle's newly-discovered verve deserted them when it mattered at Villa Park. It was a surreal atmosphere: home fans threw giant beach balls on the pitch to protest about owner Randy Lerner. It disrupted the game. Benitez implored them to build on the lessons they had learned over the previous month but Newcastle were lethargic and listless. The home fans took a day off berating their own side and taunted Newcastle, and their witless team dug in: Newcastle, who had mastered the art of counter-attack on their travels, could not set the pace. Sunderland, by contrast, crackled with intensity. Their 3-2 win over Chelsea was electrifying. They still had to win one of their two remaining games but in the second city, Newcastle knew the game was up.

Newcastle ended the season with 37 points. Benitez had done so much but it was not enough. Now the questions about his own future, that he had been deflecting for weeks, would come to a head. The appreciation for what Benitez had done was genuine. He had returned respect to the club, if not quite the points haul that had been hoped for. It really stung that Newcastle ended on 37: in that respect, Benitez had done what he'd set out to do. It was no comfort whatsoever. Sunderland's win over Chelsea was the result Benitez's calculations hadn't allowed for.

There was a break inserted in the three-year contract Benitez had signed that stipulated he could leave in the summer. He already had other offers. Friends involved with the Chinese Super League were talking about salaries in the high seven figures.

***

LEE CHARNLEY went to the Sports Direct headquarters in Shirebrook and said that if Benitez left, he would have to go, too.

Newcastle was at a crossroads but all the signs were pointing one way. *The Chronicle's* front page after the Aston Villa defeat took the form of an open letter begging him to stay. 'Everyone is right behind you and desperate for you to stay,' it read, with a picture of Benitez giving a thumbs-up super-imposed over it. A petition that accompanied it drew more than 26,000 signatures in a week. Benitez had not intended to stay on if Newcastle were in the Championship. He wanted autumn and winter under the floodlights to be in the Champions League, not at Brentford, Rotherham and Burton, fresh from League One.

The Spaniard has always been portrayed in England as the arch-pragmatist. The way Steven Gerrard depicted him in his autobiography did not do much to disprove the notion that Benitez is a cold, calculating character – more interested in winning than in relationships. 'I can pick up the phone and speak to all of my Liverpool managers, except Rafa,' he wrote. He described a 'frostiness' between the pair.

Nobody who had got to know Benitez at Newcastle would recognise that. "Maybe it is because I am a bit older, I am a bit more emotional," Benitez later reflected.

The process had begun at Anfield. His daughters, Claudia and Agata – Wirral-born, girls of the 21st century – had been monitoring social media and feeding back to their father the genuine affection that Newcastle fans had shown for him. Then they witnessed it first hand at Liverpool, the last stadium where he had been wanted, the club where a group of fans used to carry a gold framed picture of him to away games called the 'Rafatollah'. There he had won the Champions League, here he had won just one game.

After being chased out of Chelsea despite winning the Europa League, and being the man no-one seemed to want at Real Madrid, this was a different assignment. Newcastle fans were love bombing him and his family were happy to join in. "It is true, for one or two weeks my family were pushing me. [They were saying]: 'Listen, the fans love you. You have to stay. You have to stay for them," Benitez admitted afterwards.

On the final day of the season Newcastle fans might have arrived to protest the catastrophe that had landed them in the Championship for the second time in the owner's nine years in charge. A plane, paid for by Sunderland supporters, intended to rub in relegation. 'Auf weidersehen, Prem – Toon Going Down,' it read. It was ignored. Instead, the Tottenham home game turned into a referendum on Benitez: loud, lusty support for him and regular exhortations for him to stay were the order of the day. "After that, it would have been hard to walk away. It was amazing," he says. Newcastle were reduced to 10 men in the first half but still won 5-1. It could have been eight. The BBC report said it was 'like the days of Kevin Keegan'.

Charnley and Benitez had worked well together. The MD provided support, he listened. It had the beginnings of a relationship which would provide the platform for a revival. Charnley knew, deep down, that there was no way he could present an inferior, journeyman manager to Newcastle's fans and players after Benitez. It was a difficult sell to Ashley, an unpredictable owner who deals in the cold, hard currency of results.

Picture the scene at Shirebrook: Ashley had seen unprecedented funds invested in the team and the most expensive manager the club had ever employed end in relegation. This was a man who had greeted the remarkable fifth-placed finish in 2012 – a feat impressive enough to win Pardew the Manager of the Year award, remember – with a query about why he had bothered to sanction the signing of striker Cisse from Freiburg in the January, if it had not delivered the lucrative Champions League football he had been told it might. It was a serious question that – for Ashley – required an answer. It was not Benitez's emotions that presented the biggest barrier to the club's future, it was Ashley's.

But he was in attendance on the final day of the season for the

Tottenham game and shook Benitez's hand afterwards, telling him to stay. The conversation was short but the two men got on. He told Charnley to work out the details. The word from above was, "whatever Rafa wants, Rafa gets."

Benitez wanted assurances over control and to be able to run things the way he felt was necessary. Recruitment had to be left to him, which would mean changes. "The football side and the business side do not have to work against each other," he kept telling Charnley.

Changes were coming. Benitez agreed to stay. "I have responsibility for football business. I have assurances that we will have a strong, winning team," he said at his second unveiling.

Newcastle rejoiced but Benitez had been doing the sums again. History suggested that first-time promotion for teams dropping into the Championship was difficult to secure. They were immediately made the bookies' favourites on reputation alone, but three months on Tyneside had convinced Benitez that profound changes were required.

Nothing less than a revolution would suffice.

4. Without Firing A Shot

How He Won The Battle For Newcastle's Soul

"Where it went wrong? Everything started with the sofa and the lamp at Valencia. I was hoping for a sofa and they bought me a lamp"

Rafa Benitez, 2007

RAFA BENITEZ bears the battle scars of a football manager prepared to speak up when he is not handed the weapons to wage war his way. In his first really high-profile job in Spain, he went to war over a lamp when he was manager at Valencia. At Liverpool, he took up arms against unpopular American owners who had promised him the world and couldn't even deliver him a defender. The 'lamp' in question was midfielder Fabian Canobbio. Benitez had told his superiors he wanted a winger but they supplied him with a number 10. He could not hide his discontent. He spoke out. The path for a painful separation of the ways in 2004 was set.

Almost every football fan in England would be able to recall the infamous 'Facts' press conference when he was in charge at Anfield, a long, pre-prepared speech that targeted his principle rival from Manchester United, Sir Alex Ferguson. Equally as deliberate was a broadside launched at Liverpool co-owners Tom Hicks and George Gillett after they told him to stop talking about transfers and to concentrate on training the team and forthcoming games. "I am focused on training and coaching my team," he repeated, 15 times in the subsequent press conference.

It is not that he particularly seeks out confrontation or is drawn to it. But Benitez, principled and propelled by the certainty of his past success, is prepared to go into battle if he believes that his authority is being undermined or the cause is just, as it was at Anfield as he waged war against owners who he believed were damaging Liverpool. He was grateful to have the Newcastle job – but not so grateful that it undermined his ability to do the job to the best of his abilities.

In the end, though, he won the battle for Newcastle United without firing a shot. The smell of fresh paint at the training ground in the first week of June was the scent of success. The club was being coaxed back into life, one brush stroke at a time.

The last time Newcastle had been relegated, they started to cut. Jobs were made redundant as part of a streamlining process designed to cushion the club from a relegation brought on them by mistakes from the top and the lethargy of the squad. Any fears among club staff that a similar process may be sparked by this demotion were soon soothed. This time, at Benitez's insistence, they started to sow seeds.

There is an American criminology concept that was popularised in the 1980s called the 'Broken Windows Theory'. In a 1982 article for *The Atlantic*, social scientists James Wilson and George Kelling argue that preventing small anti-social crimes like public drinking and vandalism creates an atmosphere of order and lawfulness that prevents more serious problems.

"If the windows are not repaired, the tendency is for vandals to break a few more windows," they wrote. "Eventually they may even break into the building and, if it's unoccupied, maybe become squatters or light a fire."

Benitez reasoned that changes at the training ground would send a small, subtle message that the club was beginning to grow. Newcastle's training ground was hardly Alcatraz but there were little things that hadn't been improved for years. Benitez wanted the players to feel like they were part of a progressive club that was on the up: having Premier League facilities in the Championship would improve the mentality and give everyone a lift. He felt there would be the black and white equivalent of marginal gains if he could smarten it up and make it a space that people wanted to work in. It would show the players they were coming back to something different.

The paint job began with the long, dark corridors. Blues and creams lifted it out of the dull drudgery of the previous era. New lights were installed in the canteen. Sofas were bought and new video games systems installed in the players' room so that they would not be so desperate to leave the training ground. With Benitez planning double training sessions over the summer – more tactical work was planned – the manager thought it only fair. He wanted the players to talk more freely, communicate with each other and form their own bonds.

Two new synthetic pitches were laid. The dug-outs were moved to make it easier for the coaching staff. New padded seats made them more comfortable.

In his own office he asked for a mural to be painted behind his desk. It was a photo from the 1-0 defeat of Crystal Palace in the Premier League run-in – the moment, belatedly, when it all started to click for Benitez at Newcastle. It depicted brilliant blue skies over a packed St James' Park. Benitez loved it.

***

BENITEZ did not go on a long holiday in the months that followed the relegation. His time off had come in January and February – the summer had to be set aside to rebuild and re-energise a playing squad that had long since passed its sell-by date. His wife and family understood.

The scale of change over five summer weeks was incredible. No club in England did as much heavy lifting as Newcastle did over that close season.

The numbers that underpinned the revolution were nothing short of astounding; the churn of playing personnel unprecedented at a club like Newcastle. It was a summer where Newcastle signed 12 players but they also sold or released five of their 11 longest-serving players. A sixth would leave in January but, even before Cheick Tiote sealed his move to China, Newcastle had let a cumulative three decades of playing experience leave during a transformative summer. There was sorrow when he left in February, with the sense that it was the end of an era after well over six years of fine service. That was nothing compared to the profound shock and sadness when he passed at the tragically young age of 30 in June 2017, plunging the football club into mourning.

Previous managers had attempted squad overhauls but pulled back from the brink of cutting some of the club's more established players. The result had been dissatisfaction from the coaches and disquiet in the dressing room. Club captain Fabricio Coloccini had twice been close to exiting but remained at the club; his continued presence felt reluctant. The other players could sense that.

The problem for successive managers was a clear one. Sell and you risked the possibility of not finding a replacement who was up to standard. Pardew had discovered that to his cost when the club accepted bids for Demba Ba and Yohan Cabaye. Neither were effectively replaced. For a long time supporters said the same about Andy Carroll, the big, bustling, long-haired hell-raiser from Gateshead who scored goals with such frightening ease that Liverpool coughed up £35m for him. The trope that followed Newcastle for a long time during Pardew's tenure in charge was a variation on the theme of where the money that the club received for him had gone.

Benitez's hand was strong enough in negotiations to ask for two things: that he had the final say on new signings; and that there would be funds to spend on essential new players, even if Newcastle were not able to sell some of those squad players that he felt had to jettisoned.

Publicly he spoke about a third big issue that went down well with Newcastle fans. The club, he insisted, did not have to sell a single player that they did not want to. It was a message intended for the ears of the likes of Andros Townsend, Georginio Wijnaldum, Moussa Sissoko and Daryl Janmaat – four players widely tipped to move on in the summer.

Benitez was realistic about all four. He knew there was interest from Tottenham and his old club Liverpool in Wijnaldum, a talented midfielder who had been Newcastle's top scorer in his first season in the Premier League. Sissoko's advisors had been busily drumming up interest in the France midfielder for two years and he was heading for the Euros with his home country. Janmaat had been watched by Juventus but they did not feel he was good enough for Serie A. Besides, the right-back wanted to stay in England and was looking for a pay rise – just not at a Championship club. Townsend, who had enjoyed playing for Benitez, had plenty of suitors and an England place to play for.

Privately, Benitez knew it would be politically wise to allow at least three of them to leave if a decent price could be raised. Charnley had secured an agreement with Ashley over how to provide the money for the summer rebuild: an extension to the club's overdraft facility was being talked about. In the end, Ashley extended a new loan to the club of £33m. That was on top of the £129m he was already owed. It was not Benitez's money, but it was not wise to take the owner's largesse for granted. He know there may come a time in the future when failing to cover a big summer spend may be used against the manager. A huge net spend, while hanging on to players who seemed to have lost focus over the course of the relegation season, seemed unwise.

By the same token, it made no sense to publicly advertise that Newcastle were desperate sellers, keen to cover the losses of their relegation. To get the deals the club wanted, it was best to insist that they had the upper hand. He spoke to all four and told them that they had to work hard for Newcastle as long as they were still employed by the club. All four were reminded that they had played a part in relegation and owed it to Newcastle and the supporters to do their bit to return the club to the top flight. The fact that Benitez had turned down other offers to remain at Newcastle gave that some added credibility. Respect the club, the shirt and your obligations.

Their futures were important but Benitez's main focus was on building, not taking apart. Those who wanted out could wait. Player recruitment could not.

***

NOTHING is more important in football than recruitment and Newcastle had been a club defined by it from the day Ashley walked into St James' Park, and signed off on several transfer deals that had been lined up by the previous owners.

Ashley bought Newcastle without doing a thorough dive through the books, it later emerged. The waste that he inherited drove so many of the decisions that he later took. In the season Newcastle finished fifth, some of the reports that followed made it seem as if the club were just as keen to promote the fact that they had saved £400,000 on their energy bill as they were on the achievements on the pitch.

Ashley had inherited a squad full of players on big contracts that seemed only to be justified by what they had done earlier in their careers. He had not had time to study deals that were done in the months after he completed his takeover but they included the transfers of Mark Viduka, 31, from Middlesbrough, Alan Smith, 26, from Manchester United, an injury-ravaged Geremi, 28, from Chelsea and Cacapa, 30, from Lyon. All were on huge contracts. Joey Barton also joined them, from Manchester City, on a contract that, he subsequently admitted in his 2016 autobiography, included the offer of a contract to a friend to act as a PA.

The waste left Ashley disillusioned. Michael Owen's huge wages were also inherited yet the team was relegated two years later with all of those players still on the staff. For all that has fired Ashley's way since those days, he had a point.

If Newcastle were going to run efficiently, recruitment mattered and the remit was delivered from the very top. The owner, chief executive and manager shared responsibility over the transfer deals but, before they even made a phone call, the player had to tick the right boxes. They had to be the right age, have the correct salary expectation and – crucially – the potential to increase their value over time. Graham Carr oversaw a team of nine full and part-time staff at first, taking a decision that France's Ligue 1 was the best destination for Newcastle to do their shopping.

Some look back at that initial recruitment drive over the Channel and claim it was hardly rocket science, to take good internationals from a country with a rich heritage for producing good technical footballers who have been proven to settle quickly in the Premier League. But Carr had his ear to the ground about the new generation of French talent that was being hot-housed around the country. He had been tracking talent at places like Le Havre, Rennes and Troyes long before they moved on to the stages that Newcastle eventually snatched them from.

The crucial thing was that remit: informally, Newcastle did not look at anyone over the age of 26 because it was felt that their value would decline so steeply over the course of the three, four, five or even six-year contract they would be offered.

Financially, it made sense. But you only had to look at the problems that had beset Newcastle over two seasons to see where it fell down. The team had no leaders. Frequently it had no response to setbacks other than to lay down and allow another team – as Salako had said after the 5-1 Selhurst Park humiliation – to walk all over them.

Now there had to be a new direction in recruitment. Benitez had dodged questions about his relationship with long-serving chief scout Carr at his second unveiling but the latter remained in a sort of purgatory. He was prepared to accept that he would now be just one voice in recruitment rather than the main one, but no-one really knew what it would mean in practice for him. There was an understandable wariness on both sides. An invitation from Benitez to Carr to come to the club before the end of the season was turned down because he was scouting.

Benitez sensed some of that from existing club staff. The newspapers were full of talk about the 'Rafalution' by now but his message inside the club was a different one. He did not want to tear down the club from the inside. With medicine, coaching, recruitment and the Academy he wanted to engage with the people who already worked for the club.

Alongside that, Benitez had to be the driving force in terms of recruitment. As smart as some of Newcastle's buys might have been, having someone identify the players who wasn't the manager or head coach had resulted in relegation. It was completely incompatible with the way that Benitez had worked and the way he intended to operate over the long, gruelling Championship season. Benitez had to be the man charged with sourcing the players that he would coach.

***

ASK Rafa Benitez what he looks for in a player and you had better be prepared for a long answer.

These days – through slick, professional, multi-million pound companies like Italian cyber scouting firm Wyscout – footage of any player is just the click of a mouse away if you're prepared to invest five figures in a licence. Most football clubs do take the Wyscout option, opening up a global market to teams in the lower reaches of English football.

Benitez was there long before Wyscout. When he was Liverpool manager, he implored the club to invest in two giant satellite dishes at their Melwood training base. The idea was to be able to track "the big 12" – the leagues in Europe and South America that are of particular interest to Benitez.

He has a personal database that stretches to 14,000 players: past, present and future prospects looked at by scouts at all of his different clubs.

In an ideal world, Benitez would ask his scouts to watch a player between five and 10 times in the flesh. How, Benitez would enquire, would he fit into our system? Does he learn quickly? Is he prepared to sacrifice his own glory if necessary? Does he have the technical qualities? On top of that, there is personality to consider.

Benitez's former chief scout at Liverpool, Eduardo Macia, described that process in 2010: "We want to know everything about the player, not just how he performs. For example, Lucas Leiva; our scout watched him and asked lots of different people about him. Then we spent two weeks in Brazil watching him training, as well as playing.

"From that we hope to be certain about a player. Of course, you can still make a mistake but this method reduces the chances. Sometimes, even when you know everything, you still get it wrong.

"There are lots of factors to consider, such as language, wife or girlfriend not settling in a new country. You can still get it wrong, but we hope to make the least number of mistakes."

Benitez did not know the Championship, but he had started to take soundings about what the ideal Championship player looked like. One thing that came up time and time again was character. It was the one thing his Newcastle squad had been accused of not having over the previous two seasons.

Mauro Pederzoli is another former Benitez scout. He worked with him in Spain in 2007.

"There are simple but unbreakable rules that Benitez passes on to his scouts," he said, when interviewed a decade ago.

"Benitez doesn't want headline-hogging players but discipline. He avoids small players and 'fancy dans'. He looks for 'fair and strong' players. Put together those players and you get a Benitez team. His Liverpool team was a side that topped the fair play league. In one season they had no player sent off in the league."

Macia says that "strong players" are the ones that Benitez leans towards. Players who can make decisions on the pitch that "win games" are prioritised over the ones who possess individual, eye-catching ability.

Benitez remained steadfast in that belief as he constructed his Newcastle United wish-list. Character would be just as important as quality as he scoured the top two divisions and Europe's "big 12" looking for players willing to drop into the second tier with a club that would be burdened by great expectations in the 2016/17 campaign.

Owen Brown is another member of Benitez's entourage who

has proved invaluable in the past. A former manager of non-league Vauxhall Motors, the ebullient Scouser has acted in an adviser role for Benitez in his English postings and is a popular man with an impressive network of contacts. He, too, was pressed into sourcing players who would not only offer the quality required to win promotion, but also the force of personality to put a place in the top two beyond doubt.

When you look at the 12 men Benitez signed, what is remarkable is the way that the most high-profile of them have taken the road less travelled to the professional game.

He spent £22m on two players who had trekked through the lower leagues to get to the Premier League. One had spent time as a carpenter after dropping out of a Premier League academy. Another had come through a loan spell at Dagenham & Redbridge.

There is talent in Premier League academies. It is not a given that a player who has had to fight will be able to match up to what is required at a club like Newcastle. But Benitez was happy to gamble on the personalities of players who arrived at the club with hunger to prove themselves, rather than improve themselves.

Those detailed background checks were part of what was going on as Newcastle fans began to get twitchy about the lack of movement. June passed without a signing. While the training ground was being given its facelift, the foundations were being laid.

"You are not just signing pieces of furniture," Benitez says of that reconnaissance. "They have families and they have to settle. Sometimes it is not as easy as just buying a defender when you need a defender."

Most of all, Benitez wanted to get a sense that the players he was targeting understood the specific needs of being a Newcastle player. A common gripe of supporters was that the club had been used as a shop window by too many of their players.

Critics could argue that Ashley's approach would always lead to that and Benitez wanted it to change. He made an explicit promise to supporters that the days of players using Newcastle as a springboard to better things were behind them.

That element added an extra factor to the mix: making Newcastle a destination club again.

"People think that it is just about signing players and that is it," Benitez said of his approach to recruitment. "But when you have to change something, you have to change the mood around the club. You could feel that around the city, everyone was excited about the idea of being promoted again. They were talking about, 'This is our club again' and that they were proud of the team.

"They didn't see the other things we did [behind-the-scenes at the training ground] but they did see the squad. We needed to change something to ensure we had a competitive team and to bring what they call 'fresh blood' in England.

"It is difficult to bring players into the Championship. For some teams in the Championship, they have a settled squad. They need to bring in two players or maybe less to just improve their team because they know the division. The players are settled.

"When you are relegated, you lose half of the squad. Some of the best players want to leave and you have to sell them. The others, maybe they are not good enough because you have been relegated. So you keep half of the squad and bring in others."

For Benitez, it could not just be about the calibre of player. Those coming in must be able to integrate into what was left of the 2015/16 squad while also understanding what it meant to be a Newcastle player.

The club's dressing room had a reputation for being toxic. Benitez was cooking up the antidote.

5. Destroy And Rebuild

How Three Weeks In July Changed Newcastle United

"The reality is Newcastle grew radically in size the day Kevin Keegan took over. Rafa Benitez is the same – players will want to play for Rafa because he is a huge pull"

Rob Lee, 2016

EVERYONE in Newcastle knows the story. Rob Lee was one of England's finest midfield prospects, having chiselled out a reputation as a deft, intelligent creator with a knack for scoring goals. He had outgrown Charlton and had the pick of some of the most ambitious clubs in the country. Two of them, in the North East, were pushing hardest. Middlesbrough were offering a more generous financial package but then Kevin Keegan picked up the phone.

When he delights after-dinner crowds, Keegan likes to recount a joke he told Lee about Newcastle being closer to London than Middlesbrough. That clinched it, according to black and white folklore. The reality, as recalled by Lee, is different. It was Keegan, his boyhood hero, who won him over. The star quality, charisma, ambition – it gave Newcastle the edge. It had been a long time since anyone could say that about Newcastle as they hurtled towards an important transfer window. When Benitez agreed to stay, that changed in an instant. For the first time in years, that first phone call was Newcastle's greatest weapon once again.

***

BENITEZ had the cache, but he also had a strategy. It was a simple one: to strengthen the team in a way that challenged the very foundation of the club's long-standing belief that there was no value in the transfer market.

The theory that Newcastle could only make money and improve by having such good contacts, and an exquisite eye for untapped potential had brought them some fine players. But they had not had a team to speak of for two years, and they had not had a squad to share the burden of a challenging season for even longer.

Benitez knew the value of a squad. Across the first three months of the Championship season, their workload would be the equivalent to what he had experienced when he managed in the Champions League with Liverpool. There were six games in 22 days in August: Friday, Saturday, Wednesday, Saturday, Tuesday, Saturday. Six games in 18 days would be the challenge in October if Newcastle could navigate into the business end of the EFL Cup.

There would not be the bright lights of Europe's biggest stadiums, of course. Midweek assignments at Barnsley and Queens Park Rangers were early appointments – along with whatever the League Cup was going to throw at them. Benitez would rotate his players – and that meant improving them from the bottom up. At a club where funds had been restricted and the remit so prescriptive, this was revolutionary. But it made sense. Let's call it the 'weak-link theory'.

It was something I had written about in July 2016 after hearing American economist, David Sally, talking about a football book he'd penned called *The Numbers Game*. He had teamed up with an ex-professional, Chris Anderson, to investigate a theory that the sport had its priorities wrong in making superstars the most expensive and coveted assets that a club had.

"Soccer is a game where, if you get lucky and score a goal, that might just hold up. So mistakes turn out to be a very important part of soccer as a team sport," he told Malcolm Gladwell in an illuminating episode of his Revisionist History podcast. "That leads you to think mistakes often happen – or are produced – by weaker players on the pitch."

Football, he says, is a weakest link sport. Having a superb star player matters but if he drives a move that is wasted by a weakest link player who is not good enough, the ball is turned over and the chance of building towards a goal is 0 per cent. So the important thing – the thing that is going to influence a game more – is improving the 11th player, or even the bench.

Sally has spoken to Premier League chairmen about this but has found resistance. It is not glamorous and, in a world where social media has quickened the rush to judge, recruiting good players as opposed to great ones is a risky strategy. Commercially and economically it's not going to get the tills ringing.

Ashley might argue that, in the skewed transfer market, the weaker links are the least likely to appreciate in value because any improvements across a team will bolster the value of the star men first. But, as Benitez would be desperate to point out, you end up appreciating them. "Some players will be more important than the others," he explained. "But they are all part of our movement.

If we do well, they are all important." By the fourth week of the summer, the manager got to work.

***

Matt Ritchie

TEN days before Christmas, 2016. It's lunchtime on Newcastle's Quayside. Matt Ritchie is stood on the Millennium Bridge, enjoying the view and reflecting on four fantastic months as a Newcastle player with the BBC when the Christmas parties start trickling across the River Tyne towards Gateshead.

Twelve months previously, a Newcastle player would not have done it. The club wouldn't have really thought to ask – or been encouraged to. What's in it for them? It looks too risky. Who wants to stand in the cold, being grilled while punters eye you suspiciously? The public didn't know the players' stories and they didn't really want to tell them. The mistrust was mutual.

Ritchie was the new blood. Talented, of course, but that's only part of the story. Benitez had deployed him behind the number 10 in a new role that was unfamiliar from the chalk-on-the-boots winger role that he'd had at Bournemouth. It required a steep learning curve. The dividends were not immediate but here, playing out in front of the *Football Focus* cameras to the amusement of host Mark Clemmit, there was a vindication of sorts.

The first fan stops to shake his hand. He's middle-aged, good natured. A pretty typical Newcastle fan. "I really think he's been marvellous. I liked him last year, when he was at Bournemouth. There's belief in the city – it's been brilliant, I'm not watching games behind the couch anymore," he said.

And what does he think of Rafa? "If he told me it was Sunday on a Thursday, I'd believe it." Next past are a group of ladies who want autographs. It's all smiles. One offers the winger her fluffy ear muffs as he looks cold. Ritchie can't help laughing. He might have been born in Hampshire, but this feels like home.

Ask Benitez what a 'Benitez player' looks like and he'll take you through the characteristics, one by one and in sharp, forensic detail. A quicker way to explain would be to point to Ritchie, Newcastle's most important summer recruit and a man who arrived at St James' Park via the path less travelled.

Ritchie, you see, was the first name on the transfer hit-list, the blue chip name who would hit the sweet spot between Premier League class and Championship graft. In every phone call that he made to get advice on how to handle the uncharted waters he was about to take Newcastle into, Ritchie's name was the one that came up.

He'd come off the back of a good season in the Premier League but he knew the Championship. Fifteen goals in 46 games in the second tier in 2014/15 was a remarkable record from midfield.

It was the deal that Benitez knew would light the blue touchpaper for his Rafalution. "When I started people were saying: 'Oh, Rafa doesn't know the Championship.' But I was talking with a lot of people; talking about a lot of options, of different players, and Ritchie was one of the first names. He is one player that if you sign him, you know you are right."

The quality is important. But the back story is just as relevant – Ritchie's hunger for success was designed to add something to a stagnant dressing-room mix.

The scenic route, Matt Ritchie called it. Four divisions in 12 months, from living over a pub in Dagenham during a loan spell in East London to the Premier League with Bournemouth. Starting at his boyhood club, Portsmouth, he was earmarked for success after making a top-flight debut in his teenage years. But he had to drop down the divisions to make his name: first via Dagenham, where John Still first recognised the hunger in him.

"Matt was driven. I say that when players come to Dagenham,

you quickly learn whether they're made of the right stuff. We do things the right way, but it's a difficult environment if you've been in the Premier League and are used to certain things," Still told me. "Matt responded the right way. He knew what he needed to do. I can't speak highly enough of the way he applied himself."

That meant kipping in a pub for a while when he was out on loan. Next came Swindon Town and the shock tactics of Paolo Di Canio. The Italian can be a difficult character to work with, but Ritchie was fascinated by his professionalism. When Di Canio told him that his penchant for chocolate biscuits and sweets would ruin his aspirations to play international and Premier League football, he listened. Di Canio felt so strongly about Ritchie, he resigned when the winger was sold to Bournemouth.

Eddie Howe brought him on again, establishing Ritchie as a Premier League player pivotal to the Cherries' over-achievement. Days like the one at St James' Park, that brought the curtain down on the ill-fated McClaren era – one assist, a performance laced with energy – were proof Ritchie and Bournemouth belonged.

Having reached the mountain top, few would voluntarily scale back down it to take a detour. But Benitez was insistent, both to the player and to Newcastle.

When Lee Charnley returned from initial negotiations with a valuation that was greater than Benitez or Newcastle had expected, it would have spelled trouble for other managers. Recognising that Andros Townsend was set on leaving, Benitez insisted that a few million pounds were a price worth paying for a player of his qualities. Charnley acquiesced.

"We had to sell really well to have some money for buying new players but we still had to pay some (big) money for players," Benitez recalled. "In some cases, the value could be less but we still had to pay this money because we needed to sign the player. With Ritchie, Lee Charnley was phoning me to say the 'price is that' and it was not what we were expecting.

"I was saying, 'please', he is an important player, he has experience, we have to do it, we cannot be worrying about a couple of million when we have to get out of this division."

Bournemouth had a fair price but Ritchie still had to be sold on the idea of giving up his prized status as a Premier League player. There was a willingness to talk from the moment his agent, Will Salter, told him Newcastle were interested. Benitez's success and CV had opened the door to a move down a division but it was what was said next that really impressed Ritchie. Benitez had done his homework, he knew Ritchie's game inside out: where he was weak and where he could improve.

"He told me that he could teach me different styles of play," Ritchie explained in an interview with *The Journal* in February 2017. "Under Rafa I have learned that you need to be aware of what's going on in a game, how it develops and that, tactically, we are going to change match by match.

"I've been used to playing a similar way for a team throughout my career but, under this manager, we're developing different game-plans and you have to understand tactically how that works.

"It's a different style of coaching to anything I've experienced before but it's one that's very successful and makes you want to learn even more."

Learn, perform, grow. At 27 he might not be young in the football sense, but Benitez knew that Newcastle's under-26 dictat had to be broken for a player who would improve under his coaching.

Ritchie delivered 12 goals and nine assists from midfield. His impact on the club, the fans and a dressing room in which he became a leader and a talisman was even greater. Benitez had found a kindred spirit in Ritchie. He was the perfect signing.

Dwight Gayle

"TEETH", they call him. When Newcastle's number nine smiles, he flashes the molars and it's infectious. United were to see plenty of the smile over the course of the season. But when Benitez hit the phones looking for a striker who could produce 20 goals in the Championship, he heard another word to describe Gayle. Selfish.

Gayle's story began at Stansted but he began to fly at Dagenham, again under John Still. He did work with his father, Devon, on building sites to bring in a weekly wage while turning out for Saturday sides that were semi-professional. A big break arrived at Peterborough, where Barry Fry said that he was the best natural finisher he'd even met.

The upward curve was arrested at Crystal Palace. Injuries and a manager – Pardew, the man who would have been king at St James' Park – reticent to play him gave Benitez an opening.

"I had watched him play, I was aware of him long before we decided to sign him," Benitez says. "It is not always easy with a striker. In other positions, in defence or midfield, you can see that a player has to work with the team. But for strikers there is some quality from being selfish. And Dwight is selfish in the right way.

"He is a good man off-the-pitch. He does the work, he is polite, respectful. He wants to learn. But he has the qualities of a striker – he will work hard, he wants goals and he is selfish like that.

"I spoke to people who had worked with him and they said that he is a worker. All of the information was positive. If he has to work on the training ground on something, he will do it."

On the day Newcastle were handing out squad numbers, the manager had set up a finishing school to decide between him and Aleksandar Mitrovic as to who would take a number nine journey which both wanted. The former shirt of Alan Shearer, Jackie Milburn and Malcolm Macdonald, it has extra cache. When Shearer signed, it was a condition of the £15m move. Gayle had cost £12m – hardly small change for a relegated side – but he was not guaranteed it. Mitrovic, eventually, stepped aside. He could see what it meant to Gayle to join those names.

Benitez's praise for Gayle is sincere. "If you ask him to do something, he will do it. If you ask him to make a movement, which means he helps the team but maybe sacrifices himself, he will do it, no problem.

"He has a really positive attitude. When you look for quality and he is a good finisher, that is great but it helps hugely that he is a good character and has the right mentality, too.

"That is what we are looking for at Newcastle now. Dwight is perfect for that. He is someone who wants to improve. You cannot put a price on that."

He signed on the same day as Ritchie: July 1. Benitez had his two figureheads. Matz Sels, a Belgian goalkeeper recommended by Graham Carr, was a surprise acquisition three days before to cover the absence of Rob Elliot – the club's best goalkeeper – and Tim Krul, the club's most naturally talented stopper but who had injury problems.

Sels had been Belgium's third-choice going into the Euros. He arrived from Gent with the same hard-working attitude that the other two possessed. Benitez had persuaded Newcastle to sign a fifth goalkeeper to their books – a move intended to provide insurance against long-term injuries but also competition for Karl Darlow, a player that Benitez seemed to need convincing of.

Jesus Gamez, from Atletico Madrid, made it four new arrivals within a week. He was an experienced player intended to imbue professionalism in the squad and – again – to offer competition among defenders. He did not play much. Benitez would probably admit that it took Gamez longer to adapt than expected.

Isaac Hayden

ISAAC HAYDEN heard the snap in his right ankle as soon as Mathieu Flamini did it. Ligaments ripped, a dream dead. He was in the Arsenal team to play Hull City at the Emirates on the Saturday – a reward for years of diligent work at Arsenal's Hale End Academy, patiently tracked by Arsene Wenger.

Hayden walked off in agony. It was a micro fracture of the ankle ligaments – months out. He told the physios he was OK, popped a few pain killers and hoped that he might be able to play through the excruciating pain. The delusion lasted an hour before he called for his girlfriend to help him up the stairs and back to bed.

When Rafa Benitez remodelled Newcastle's midfield, he wanted someone to bridge the gap between Jonjo Shelvey's creativity and Jack Colback's industry. Hayden fitted the bill perfectly – the background call between Wenger and Benitez revealed the warmth the Frenchman felt for Hayden. He described him as a sponge, always willing to listen and learn.

Newcastle faced competition. Premier League clubs wanted him but Hayden only needed to hear Benitez talk about his game and his vision for improving it – he had a detailed speech for every potential signing that summer – to know it was the right move.

Benitez's vision involved Premier League football. It involved a 'project' for next season and beyond. "I didn't think this club just wanted to stay in the Premier League," he says, of that initial talk with Benitez. Every interview he gives, Hayden will repeat the 'L' word: learning. "Some things he says, you sit, think and say, 'Oh, OK', and it hits you afterwards. It's incredible. It's not about perfection – you can never reach that level – but he is a perfectionist. Every detail has to be correct." Hayden signed on July 11. Newcastle had strengthened their spine with a striker, midfielder and two defenders, just as Benitez said they would.

Mo Diame

MO DIAME remembers exactly where he was when he was told to stop playing football. He had just earned his first professional contract for Ligue 1 side Lens, a weekly wage that he would send back to Creteil, to support a family devastated by the loss of his father from cancer. The message was not advisory. He was told not to kick a ball again until further notice. No exercise, no football, no future in the game.

A latent cardiac problem meant that doctors for Lens could not guarantee his safety if he took to the pitch. It was devastating, incredible news for a man who had rubbed shoulders with French football's golden generation at Clairefontaine, the talent factory that created a nation of sporting heroes.

Diame told Lens he would play anyway. They refused. A year in exile became unbearable. He demanded they rip up his contract and moved to Spain, to the only club that would take a chance on him: CD Linares, an Andalusian Second Division team with such a minute budget that they had to think outside the box.

Diame played well but the shrinking budget disappeared. For three months over Christmas he went unpaid, along with the rest of the squad. Recalling it is the only time his smile fades.

Benitez wanted character but also balance. He did not play with a number 10 in the traditional sense, but he wanted someone who could move in between the lines of a striker and a midfielder.

He had an option in his squad in Siem de Jong, the talented but frail ex-Ajax forward. He liked him, much as he liked Florian Thauvin. One was unreliable, the other lacked motivation.

Diame dropped down a division, another lured by the promise of playing under Benitez. Hull had offered him a new contract but the Spaniard talked of a project to turn Newcastle into a force in England again. He laid it out for Diame, season-by-season. A year in the Championship, establishing themselves in the Premier League and then challenging for Europe again. It was not a pipe dream: Benitez had backed it up with specifics.

There was a release clause in Diame's contract. Other Premier League clubs knew but Benitez's sales pitch edged it. Diame did not regret it.

Daryl Murphy

WHEN Benitez's team of scouts, fixers and advisors reflected on the work they had done in summer 2016, they got to talking about another consequence of their flurry of transfer activity. By pushing Newcastle's Championship cause, they had also weakened others in the division. It was an intended chain reaction of them re-investing in the transfer market, to pick off the best of the rest.

Ciaran Clark arrived from Aston Villa, the club exploiting a clause in his contract that allowed them to sign him from his boyhood side – but a place where he'd grown stale. Benitez recognised a player seeking a new challenge. He ignored his performances in a team that had been relegated and looked for the potential.

Newcastle also paid around £5.5m for Blackburn's Grant Hanley. It was the sort of deal the club would never have done before Benitez's arrival: a second international centre-back through the door to increase competition. Again, a rival had been weakened.

They had dreamt that they could do the same to Brighton by providing Anthony Knockaert with an alternative to the south coast but ran into an obstruction in the form of the Seagulls' ambitious, professional-gambler owner, Tony Bloom. He simply would not countenance selling the French winger, who might have added a dash of creativity and verve to a side that – Benitez grew to understand – required a bit more unpredictability.

The longer the window went on, the more practical the club had to become. More firepower was required to mitigate the unpredictable Mitrovic and maturing Ayoze Perez. Gayle could be relied upon but they still felt short. The budget was stretched. Newcastle had two attacking options in mind: Murphy or Rickie Lambert, the former Liverpool, Southampton and West Brom veteran. Carr was asked his opinion.

The goals record of the two diverged significantly. Lambert had scored three in the Premier League in two years. Murphy, in contrast, had netted 50 Championship strikes in three years. He also had a five-year stint at Sunderland on his CV. Having been denied a few million to land brighter Ligue 1 stars in the past, it must have irked Carr to see a potential £3.5m being spent on a 35-year-old forward.

Benitez knew what he was doing. Supporters were puzzled. Some Sunderland fans rejoiced at the Murphy signing as proof of how far Newcastle had fallen. But Benitez was picking from a shallow pool of genuinely capable forwards with the right attitude and attributes to play the role. Murphy was prepared to sign without assurances. He had the selfishness of a striker, but an ego that was malleable enough to accept the selection policy of a manager who did not intend to make him his starting forward. It turned out to be an incredibly shrewd bit of business.

Ciaran Clark

CIARAN CLARK had a vision for his career. He wanted to be Aston Villa captain by the age of 30 – the fulfilment of a boyhood dream at the club he'd been at since the age of nine.

Sometimes, the cold, hard reality checks the dream. Aston Villa's downfall had been even more pronounced than Newcastle's: Clark was collateral. His performances had been dragged down by the morass that surrounded him. Villa's relegation meant that he was obliged to take a 50 per cent wage cut.

Benitez's background calls all told the same story about Clark: reliable, a fighter. Look beyond a campaign at Villa Park where no-one came out of it with credit. Some supporters were far from enthusiastic but Benitez liked what he saw.

The feeling was mutual. There was momentum at Newcastle. Clark liked the look of the signings they'd already made. When Benitez talked him through how his defensive unit would play, Clark liked the way it sounded. At 26, he still had plenty to learn.

"A no brainer," he said of the decision later. At £5m, Clark was arguably Newcastle's best value signing of the summer. Benitez would have paid much more, but knew of the release clause that allowed him to talk to other clubs.

He was not looking to move on. Loyalty was his first instinct. But it was Villa's misfortune that Newcastle were the club that came calling. It was a very shrewd move.

***

IN total there were 12 additions to the squad. Newcastle had a right-back of sorts in Vurnon Anita but Benitez, remembering the nightmare that he inherited, moved to sign an American full-back, DeAndre Yedlin, from Tottenham. He arrived via a spell in Wearside at Sunderland, well aware of the North East's charm.

Benitez felt Newcastle were two wingers short but they only signed one: Christian Atsu, a loan capture from Chelsea. His cameo roles were not regular but they were important. He scored the crucial second goal against Preston that eased nerves when Newcastle were wobbling. His brilliant free-kick at Cardiff sealed Newcastle's record-breaking 14th away win.

Achraf Lazaar was a £3m capture from Palermo. The left-back played only four times, but the improvement in the man he was challenging – Paul Dummett – was clear. There was debate about some of the additions, but there was a purpose and direction to Newcastle's recruitment. As Benitez would tell those who questioned his approach, the level of the existing players improved because of the players who came in.

Not every signing had to be a stunning success. There was a bigger idea at play. After Newcastle's recruitment failings, Benitez bringing his football knowledge to play made perfect sense.

6. Peace In Our Tyne

Winning Hearts And Minds

"Football means so much in this region. It's so important that they get back into the Premier League. It's got this fantastic support that will carry on following them through whatever"

Kevin Keegan, 2017

THE smell of grilled burgers wafted over Newcastle's Academy training pitches. The excited voices of the primary school children decked in black and white battled with the noise from the PA that blasted out Calvin Harris.

Rafa Benitez had come to Newcastle to win silverware but the 1892 Foundation Cup was the first trophy lifted on his watch. A community tournament pulled together in a few days, it might have been the club's most important trophy of the season. Benitez was ensuring Newcastle had a team: now it needed the scene. "When I arrived at Newcastle, I sensed a distance between the fans and the club," Benitez said, a year on from his unveiling as United manager.

As much as the absence of a fit left-back, a loud enough whistle or a squad with enough balance to cope with the challenge of fighting a Premier League survival battle, this concerned the man tasked with restoring a club that had slowly, inexorably, pivoted away from its public.

Benitez recognised the enthusiasm for the club. It was difficult to miss in the way people talked to him about Newcastle United when he met them. The most frequent phrase that he heard from fans was "thank you". Supporters who had been desperate for something in black and white that they could believe in felt he represented it. They believed in the idea of a football club that unified the city and that they could be proud of, but they now saw nothing in the modern Newcastle to actually back that up.

As much as Benitez might have appreciated the faith that people had in him, he knew that was wrong. Benitez's experience at Liverpool illustrated the importance of the community role of a football club. He had been moved to tears listening to the stories of the Hillsborough survivors and the families of the victims of that awful day in April 1989. The city, the football club, had supported them when it felt like swathes of the rest of the country just wanted them to quietly drop their campaign.

Poignantly, Benitez donated £96,000 to the Hillsborough justice campaign when he left Liverpool in 2010.

Benitez loved the pride that Scousers had in their city. The football club was an extension of that. Barcelona might have swiped the phrase, 'Mes Que Un Club' – more than a club – for their Nike-branded t-shirts but, in Benitez's view, it had to apply to every football club. They do not stand in isolation from the city around them. In England, he had learned that lesson from his time with Liverpool. Benitez said he "smelled football" from the moment he walked into the city of Newcastle, too.

"It is a hard-working city," he said. He was able to appreciate what Kevin Keegan had noted in March of the 2016/17 promotion season on a return to the city – that people left a defeat swearing that they would not return the following week but, by the Wednesday, they had reversed that decision and were ready to offer absolute support again.

Mike Ashley had tested that loyalty, time and time again. In a rare public intervention before Newcastle's crucial relegation game against West Ham in 2015, he had insisted that his continued reason for owning the club was to deliver silverware but his words were not backed up by actions.

Ashley's modus operandi had been to act without explanation. He did not engage and those who worked for him, on behalf of the club, did not always offer reasons for what had been done. When Joe Kinnear was brought back for a second spell as director of football after years out of the game, it disillusioned those who cared about the club's credibility. Kinnear had publicly insulted Alan Shearer and repeated some lazy stereotypes about the club after his first spell. Bringing him back just two years after that was not just a blow to those who hoped Newcastle could compete with the country's leading clubs, it was also flying in the face of the sensibilities of Tyneside.

Ashley's fingers had seemed to have been burnt by Keegan's third coming. If you speak to people who know Ashley, they will tell you he is a likeable man who applies razor-sharp logic to problems when they are put to him. He approaches football problems with the sharp eye of a ruthless businessman. Many who have met him through the corporate ties at Newcastle even say he is warm and funny. But there were too many indignities on his watch for the majority to hand him the benefit of the doubt.

The owner was also captivated by the idea that the media

should pay for access to his football club. He saw pages and pages of newspapers – national and local – filled by the Premier League and felt that they were using that product to sell their own.

Sky, whose Sports News channel has always been the closest to him and his hierarchy, paid billions for access. Why were these organs allowed free access?

He had butted heads with newspapers in the past. *The Chronicle* was banned for two years for reporting on a protest against him that followed Kinnear's appointment. The club felt it was the latest in a line of coverage that lacked balance and was partisan. They cited the headline, 'March if you want Ashley out' as proof of the editorial line. The ban was levied before a Wear-Tyne derby at the Stadium of Light that Newcastle lost 2-1. Alan Pardew was prevented from answering questions from the local journalists, exposing the decision to ban – which had not been made public before then.

Local newspaper circulation might be on the decline, but authority of their reporters is not. The digital audience for local news organisations is bigger than even the days when privileged access to the team meant travelling with the players on the bus, picking up their foibles and secrets. Through Twitter, direct access from readers gives an opportunity to pass instant judgements and it also provides a relationship with the writer that has fostered the sort of accountability that was perhaps missing in a previous, supposedly golden generation of journalism.

You wouldn't expect Ashley or his men at Newcastle to track these trends. They didn't seem particularly interested in the changing landscape of the media and they had banned other journalists who had written critical stories. *The Telegraph* was excluded twice, the first time for reporting on dressing room frictions that were later confirmed by a player who had moved on.

Ashley wanted to monetise access. Preferential treatment in terms of exclusive player interviews was the currency used as a bargaining chip. It might have made business sense but it risked alienating other reporters, who were unlikely to take this challenge to their profession sitting down. The club might have ridden that storm, but it showed precious little regard for the players or manager who would have to deal with the fall-out. When McClaren's unveiling was limited to one newspaper it damaged him deeply. It was another example of the club failing to realise what an unnecessary intervention they had made.

It felt like tit-for-tat when the club, in a move supposedly made to save money, withdrew hot food from the press room on matchdays. Some fans rightly pointed out to indignation as looking a bit rich from spoiled journalists who shouldn't expect to be fed before matches. It was not the point: the food on offer was to visiting journalists as well, who had always associated a trip to Newcastle with a visit to a club that was warm, friendly and embraced visitors. That is how the city treats those who visit: a reputation that everyone wanted to preserve. Some of the hospitality staff in the press room – among the friendliest faces you could wish to meet – were distraught. It sent the wrong message.

These were the problems that Benitez was inheriting. McClaren had drawn together journalists just after his appointment and asked what the problem was. He said that he sensed the antagonism on both sides and wanted to bridge the gap. His concerns fell on deaf ears. When asked what he had changed he said that he had managed to get tea and biscuits put on in the press room. He meant that he was making incremental progress while working on the big issues. But the deep, fundamental shift in attitude was not forthcoming. Benitez, by contrast, was able to fast-track the changes, through force of personality.

The lazy assumption that Ashley was doomed because he was from London or Newcastle's fans expected too much was beginning to evaporate, too. Sky had televised the game at which many fans stayed away in protest at the club's attitude to them and, while some had seen another example of a supporter base disenchanted because the team was not challenging at the top of the table, Jamie Carragher blew through the bluster with an evisceration of Ashley's leadership live on Sky.

He was asked whether the boycotting fans were harming the team. "It won't help the team on the pitch, but the supporters have tried all sorts and, whatever they're thinking of doing, that's the only thing left for them.

"Newcastle, we always talk about how long they've gone without a trophy, so it's not as if everybody expects, 'We should win this and we should win that'.

"The fans know their club better than us. The thing as a supporter is, even if you're not going to win, you want to have the hope that something could happen.

"If you're paying for your season ticket you're hoping that someone upstairs has that same hope and belief that something could happen. Nobody expects to win a trophy – especially Newcastle – every season but they want to have the hope that something could happen.

"That's just been killed at that club because of Mike Ashley."

It was a staggering statement. It was not a new opinion to those on Tyneside who had been talking about these issues for years but to hear someone high-profile, and with no affiliation to the club, saying it was fresh. The protests seemed to be working.

Benitez recognised this. He recognised the cynicism and hurt among Newcastle fans but also – crucially – he saw how it was affecting the club's staff. "We have so many good people at this club," Benitez had said during the promotion season. Although it was billed as a 'Rafalution', it was about more than just one man.

It was not a club with a huge staff of people parachuted in from elsewhere. The majority of the club's staff support Newcastle and have done for generations. They loved the club it was not always easy to feel proud of it. That had to change.

***

THE idea behind the 1892 Foundation Cup was simple.

Benitez wanted to send a message that the club was community-facing again. He had spoken to the club's hard-working Foundation and asked what it could do – what he could do specifically. His proposal was simple: football. A five-a-side tournament, to be played every year. Inner-city schools, boys and girls, invite the parents and he would give his support. But he knew it was down to the people who worked at the Foundation and the Academy to make a success of it. A bit of faith and support went a long way.

When the children arrived at the Academy, bused-in on a summer's afternoon, excited, they walked into the dressing room to see black and white shirts on the pegs for them. The new kit was not available in shops yet, but each and every one of them had been given one to play in that afternoon. It was a classy touch.

About halfway through the day, the heaven's opened. The sheet rain forced parents to dash for cover. A summer's day in Newcastle. But the warmth was genuine.

Benitez was leading a second training session for the senior players at the first team training headquarters while the 1892 Cup was being played out but, after he'd finished, he walked over to the Academy pitches with a smile on his face. He was followed by first-team players: Paul Dummett, captain Jamaal Lascelles and the children's favourite, Aleksandar Mitrovic, a smiling presence among the throng of excited youngsters.

They handed out trophies and signed autographs. The whole event was flung open to some of the same journalists who had been banned a year or two before. They were subtly reminded to note the purpose of the day and not just to run quotes from Benitez about transfers. It worked better than the biscuits and hot drinks. It made the front page of *The Chronicle*. A little bit of love went a long way.

"This will live with the children forever," Benitez said after he'd finished posing for autographs. There was a genuine emotion in his voice.

***

SOMETIMES, the secret is just to show up. It was a lesson the club's Foundation had to learn the hard way in May 2015.

The banqueting suite had been booked, the winners announced and the plans put in place for the club's annual end-of-season awards. A black tie event in conjunction with local businesses, the idea had been to celebrate the best of black and white and pour money into Foundation projects, which would help some of the city's most vulnerable: those for whom the football club was a lifeline off the pitch as well as on it. Hours of work had been poured into organising it.

However, as results worsened, the club were faced with a stark choice: could the team be seen to be celebrating while relegation was on the cards?

Word got out. On May 14, with the club's Premier League survival in the balance, so did a statement:

'Newcastle United Football Club has made the very difficult decision that in view of the current league position, it would not be appropriate for the team and coaching staff to be celebrating the season and collecting awards at a time when our only focus is on the next two games and securing Premier League status.

'The Club would like to extend its apologies for any inconvenience caused to those businesses who had purchased tables to support the event, but we hope that you can appreciate our decision has not been taken lightly.

'The Club will work with the Foundation to find another opportunity to support them to raise funds for their outstanding work, which engages with over 50,000 people in our community.'

The decision was not taken lightly. There was genuine anguish among people at the club who had worked hard to put it on. But Newcastle had become a club that was ashamed of showing its own face. Benitez's presence changed all of that.

There was rarely a day during the season when his work began after 7am but he found time. Club staff soon learned that he was receptive to requests to show his face or lend support.

He had spoken about the club needing to re-engage, but the buck stopped and started with him. And that meant not ignoring the small stuff.

Premier League Kicks is one of those initiatives that never makes the back pages of the newspapers. It rarely makes the inside either. It was set up and funded by the Premier League to use football as a way of breaking down barriers in communities.

Everybody talks about football's social responsibility – on a Friday night, at 12 venues across Newcastle 48 times a year, it plays out in real time. At a time when social cohesion is being threatened from all angles, it is exactly the sort of thing football clubs, with the ability to influence, should be doing. And it works.

When the Foundation manager, Steve Mack, says that it is the focus of many of the young people who turn up, he really means it. You would not think the same would apply for one of the world's most decorated managers, especially not the night before a home match that his team have to win. But at 7pm on October 14, Benitez showed up at the SoccerWorld football centre in Westgate. He brought captain Jamaal Lascelles with him.

The Kicks regulars did not know he was coming. The wide-eyed astonishment was a testament of Newcastle United's capacity to make a difference. One after the other, the pair posed for pictures and autographs.

These boys were from a part of the city a million miles away from the world that Benitez inhabited but when he was asked what he'd made of the night, he noted the one thing that united them. "Their love of football brought them here," he said. The same was true of Benitez.

***

ON a day off, Benitez and his coaching staff visited the cities' landmarks. He wanted a sense of the heritage. He walked to the top of the castle that gave the city its name. He stood under the Angel of the North; visited Durham Cathedral and castle. No other manager had ever done that. Benitez, discreetly, asked about small local charities that he and his wife could help.

He was told about the Sir Bobby Robson Foundation. Set up in 2008, it has raised more than £10m through the work of ordinary volunteers. Sir Bobby was terminally ill when he opened it, a typically selfless and heroic act from a man who recognised the transformative power of the region's most popular sport.

Benitez had assumed the charity was a big operation, but it's not. There are no full-time fundraisers. It relies on good will and reputation. So he paid a low-key visit to the Freeman Hospital's Northern Centre for Cancer Care – the North East's centre of excellence in the battle against cancer.

Robson's charisma contributed to the charity, which is his legacy. Although Newcastle manager, Sir Bobby cut through the region's tribal sporting rivalries. The final game he watched was at Sunderland. He spoke of the difference the centre and the innovation of its trials centre could make to everyone, regardless of their colours.

As a member of the public you have to hope that you never have to make the short journey from the Freeman Hospital to the centre but, if you do, you walk past 'The Football Corridor' to get there. Pictures of Sir Bobby's career and football adorn the walls. Benitez was met by Liz Luff, Newcastle fan and tireless champion of the Foundation. "As we were getting into the car to leave, the first thing I blurted out to him was, 'Thank you for rescuing my football club'," she remembers. "I just had to say something." Liz loved Sir Bobby.

She was touched when previous Newcastle manager, Chris Hughton, decided to put a framed picture of Sir Bobby in the manager's office. Benitez moved it – to the entrance of the training ground where everyone who walked in would see it.

"That choked me up. When he came to the centre he was exactly what I hoped he would be," Liz said.

Benitez's guide that day was Lady Elsie Robson, Sir Bobby's widow. There was a moving meeting with Professor Ruth Plummer. They spoke at length. He wanted to know more about what the centre did. Lady Elsie recognised a kindred spirit with her beloved husband.

Benitez took time to take everything in. Over a cup of tea, he joked about the ways he managed to "cheat" his wife into watching football when they went out or on holiday. Lady Elsie nodded. She knew what he meant.

Liz said: "Newcastle is a one-club city. It's a club that means so much to the people and I think, to some people, that can seem a bit suffocating but Rafa seemed so at ease with it."

She wrote a piece about it for *True Faith* that included a lovely anecdote. "As we were leaving the Northern Centre for Cancer Care a man in a wheelchair, obviously keen to be discharged, came up behind Rafa and shouted loudly in broad Geordie: 'Howay man Rafa. Oot the way. Ah wanna gan hyem!'

"I have no idea if he understood the words, but I'm sure he understood the tone. He's already one of us."

Indeed, Benitez talked about it for days afterwards. He asked what more he could do. It was not a flesh pressing exercise.

A few days later, he was the star guest at the Foundation's Annual Awards dinner. Under the bright lights at St James' Park, there were tears and applause as hard-working volunteers and the brightest and most engaged were celebrated. Every single member of the first-team squad was told to attend. None skipped it.

The excited chatter and sense of optimism that night warmed the heart on a winter's night of typically bracing Tyneside cold. Newcastle were winning matches and friends.

***

HE can't quite pinpoint the moment it went, but it was a warm May afternoon in 1995 when Steven Farrell first fell in love with Newcastle United.

His dad, Kevin, a Sunderland supporter, had finally admitted defeat. Sending him to a primary school full of Newcastle fans in the middle of the most exciting period in the club's history meant he would not be following his father to Roker Park.

Kevin Keegan's Newcastle were three-up inside 30 minutes. Keith Gillespie's third goal was a chip so deft it belonged in the city's Laing Art Gallery.

Farrell stood in the Gallowgate paddock. It felt like he belonged. Newcastle were also the cause for his first heartbreak. Nearly a year later, Kevin had managed to get tickets for the Manchester United match – "I don't know how, it was packed out," Farrell recalls – that was settled by Eric Cantona's half-volley.

"I remember that, at the end of the game, I thought, 'We'll be OK.' We still had a point on them. But I looked around and there were all these older guys just absolutely gutted, with their heads in their hands. It looked like there'd been a bereavement," he says.

"March 4, 1996. Of course, we all know what happened next. When we didn't do it at the end of that 1995/96 season I just felt totally heartbroken."

Matchdays evolved. Friends and family, drinks, food, but always the match on a Saturday afternoon.

"I just love matchdays. I know fans at other clubs absolutely hate hearing Newcastle United supporters talk about the club being unique – and I understand that – but there's a feeling in the city on a Saturday afternoon that is just different.

"It's a one-club city so I think that makes a difference. I live in Low Fell in Gateshead, 10 minutes from town and you're right into the centre of it on matchday. The stadium dominates the city, the match is on everyone's mind. It's the fans mingling with the shoppers and the families, the scarves, the atmosphere. As soon as you get into town you feel that anticipation."

It had been that way for 20 years. Plenty of thick at the start, more thin by the end. Keegan was the spark and Sir Bobby Robson kept the flame burning before Graeme Souness and Sam Allardyce tested patience. The football was risible but supporting is an unbreakable bond, isn't it?

"Right up until the end of the 2014/15 season, I was still going the game with my mates. But the club just became this cold, unfeeling thing to us.

"They didn't care, it felt like they didn't really want us there. Alan Pardew was the manager and it was so hard to warm to him. I sometimes watched him on TV and I felt sorry for him because he always had this hangdog look on his face.

"But then there was the David Meyler thing [Pardew headbutted Meyler on the touchline at Hull, picking up a £100,000 fine], the Manuel Pellegrini thing [Pardew called the Manchester City manager a 'f***ing old c**t' on the sidelines, prompting more FA censure]. The things he said – you just became embarrassed at the way the club was representing itself.

"This was after renaming the ground after Mike Ashley's company, (pay day lender) Wonga as the shirt sponsor, Keegan being messed around, Joe Kinnear – twice. I think it was worse in that last year. The club's Twitter feed was this cold, unfeeling thing – they just tweeted out adverts for club tat. They never explained, never talked. I just felt it wasn't the club I fell in love with.

"I remember sitting there, watching this pretty poor football under John Carver, and thinking: 'Why am I paying £520 to put myself through this?'"

There was one last hurrah. Newcastle beat West Ham 2-0, Jonas Gutierrez scoring the second goal in the year he'd gone through chemotherapy for testicular cancer. Farrell and his friends hugged, celebrating that goal as hard as any during the club's glory days. By then, he'd decided not to renew his season ticket. "It was a really hard decision, but I just couldn't," he said.

The first Saturday of the new season felt odd. "It was a void. I kept telling people I wasn't missing it but I did. It was about taking a stand really – I didn't want the club to keep doing what it was doing and just expect me to put up with it because of loyalty. But I missed it, even though the team was losing. Shopping, watching TV on the Saturday. It wasn't the same."

When Rafa Benitez took over as manager, that feeling changed. "The stuff he was saying, the way he talked about the club, it was the same sort of warmth that you had from Kevin Keegan and Sir Bobby Robson.

"I don't know how to describe it. We didn't stay up but he had a dignity about him and the way he talked about Newcastle. He didn't need to be there. He'd have had loads of better offers but he wasn't just doing it for a line on his CV. It felt like he wanted to be there."

Farrell missed the final day of the season against Spurs. He was at a family occasion but found a TV showing the game. It looked like what he remembered Newcastle was.

"I came back and said to my wife Helen: 'I'm going to go back.' She understood," he said.

Farrell wasn't the only one. Newcastle had spent successive summers fighting a rearguard action against supporters not renewing their season tickets. The tickets – laudably – were always affordable, the club's reasonable pricing being one of the few things they got right during those barren years. But, even then, they were still a hard sell.

The club that had a waiting list took to sending out letters to fans urging them to come back. One year, a letter from McClaren promising investment and a team that would be competitive was mailed out to try and persuade the doubters.

The queues that snaked out of the club's box office on the day season tickets went on general sale after Benitez agreed to stay told their own story. Farrell was one of an extra 3,500 season tickets Newcastle sold for the Championship. Many more turned up on matchdays.

Newcastle's average crowd pushed over 51,000. They sold out St James' Park eight times. They were only the second club in the history of the division to record an average gate of more than 50,000. The reason? Rafa.

"When Keegan was manager, he could have sat there and just coughed into the microphone and I would have listened.

"I got the opportunity to meet him at the Baltic for an entrepreneur's forum organised through work. My boss asked me if I wanted to meet him. I mean, talk about a question that doesn't need answering.

"He stood and talked to me for half an hour. I mentioned my wife in passing at one point and, when he finished talking to me, he said: 'Pass my love on to Helen.' Some people, you feel they're not actually listening to you when they speak to you. He must have spoken to hundreds of people that night, but he was listening to everyone. He was bothered.

"Rafa is the first person since then who makes you feel like that about the football club. It's not about reacting to everything the fans want, it's about feeling like they know what the point of existing is. It's meant to be fun, it's meant to be something you can be proud of. I think Rafa knows that. You know he does."

When the season kicked-off on August 5, Newcastle were followed by 7,000 fans to Fulham. The game against Huddersfield Town on August 13 was sold out. Things were building while Newcastle were beginning to take shape.

7. Crash Landing

The Rafalution Stalls – But Only For A Fortnight

"Everybody was saying: 'You have lost your first two games. This is bad'. I never thought it was that bad. We were playing well"

Rafa Benitez, 2016

FABRICIO COLOCCINI was tired. Not physically: he had not kicked a ball competitively since February, his hamstring injury laying waste to any hope that Benitez had of coaxing season-saving performances out of Newcastle's skipper.

Mentally, he felt drained. Newcastle had squeezed the best out of him over the course of nearly a decade on Tyneside – and also the worst. Eight years after signing for Newcastle, via the ill-fated transfer committee that so put Kevin Keegan on edge, and without a word of English in his vocabulary, he had invested more in the club than he ever thought he would.

Newcastle was sold to him as a destination, a gateway to the Premier League. It ended up being the stop that defined his professional life – and in June 2016, that had to come to an end.

Newcastle made the hideous mistake of not spotting that sooner. They fought to keep the captain when he tried to leave, citing homesickness, in 2012. Their best player, a talisman and influencer for a dressing room of nations, attempted to engineer a move back to his boyhood club, San Lorenzo, and fans saw it as a betrayal. Coloccini woefully misjudged the mood and his power play backfired, but his form mitigated some of those supporter reservations in the following years.

By the time Newcastle snuck out news of his two-year contract extension, minutes before a McClaren press conference in 2015, it was the unvarnished act of a desperate club. They had scoured Europe for a replacement for Coloccini, who had been kept out of pre-season action on the assumption that he would leave. Crystal Palace and a reunion with Pardew was a distinct possibility.

But Newcastle sized up the options, priced up the cost of a Coloccini deal and fatally undermined McClaren. Carr had put forward Joel Matip, an ambitious target who ended up at Liverpool. McClaren wanted Richard Keogh, a more prosaic target who would have jumped at the chance to leave Derby. He had to retain Coloccini and, in the interests of balancing the dressing room, he had to keep the captain's armband.

The message it had sent to the squad and fans reverberated. Coloccini had been one of the finest centre-backs in England. His performance in a Wear-Tyne derby moved Pardew to compare him to Bobby Moore, that most elegant of defenders, and there was something of that to his play – when the mood took him.

He was also moody and sullen at times. For a captain, his lack of visibility irked the North East press corps and concerned the supporters. Infamously, he led a dressing room backlash against Pardew-inspired plans to fine Yohan Cabaye for his wildcat strike following interest from Arsenal, which he was not allowed to follow up. Coloccini spoke out on the French midfielder's behalf, making it difficult for Pardew to carry the dressing room.

He got on well with the owner, and had gone to dinner with him on several occasions. He held off on signing a contract because he wanted assurances from above that Newcastle had the ambition to challenge the top six consistently. He got them but there was a lingering sense of disappointment at what happened after, with Coloccini feeling his chance to speak to bigger clubs when his contract was running down was taken away from him by broken promises. Sometimes, he applied himself that way on the field.

Benitez would not make the same mistake. The captaincy was not the issue but the need for his dressing room to be purged of cynicism and reluctance was pressing. The pair shook on it, Benitez called Charnley and an exit plan was prepared. The final year of one of the most ill-advised contract extensions Newcastle had ever offered was terminated by mutual consent.

'It might be time to let others arrive with the same drive, impetus and desire as I did eight years ago,' Coloccini wrote in an open letter to the supporters after his move to San Lorenzo was finally completed. The timing might not have been perfect, but the sentiment was. Newcastle's Rafalution had its first casualty.

***

IN total, Benitez sacrificed six of the 11 longest-serving players that he inherited over the course of the promotion season. No other Newcastle manager had made so many changes in such a short space of time in the modern era.

None of them left without a handshake or a call from the manager to thank them for their efforts. In truth, he was happy for almost all of them to leave – either to prevent distractions for a group that he wanted to concentrate on the job in hand, or because they had passed their sell-by date. It was a cull that should have materialised months before.

Papiss Cisse vacated the number nine shirt: a five-year rollercoaster spell brought to an end with a move to China. The enduring image of his time with Newcastle was his gravity-defying goal of the season at Stamford Bridge – an incredible high that he could not replicate. He had stayed for two years too many.

Steven Taylor was allowed to leave on a free, the final link to Sir Bobby Robson's tenure broken. The rich potential that once persuaded the club to make him one of their highest earners was never truly fulfilled. His desire on the pitch was not questioned, but Benitez – again – felt a break was required from the past.

Wijnaldum got his move to Liverpool and Janmaat transferred to Watford after the season had started. Andros Townsend departed for Crystal Palace with a handshake. Benitez's attitude to Sissoko, France's outstanding player in a Euro 2016 they ended as beaten finalists, was more curious. He posed as many problems as Coloccini. Divisive and desperate to leave, he had offended the club and its supporters with an interview on the eve of the finals re-stating his desire to depart for a Premier League club. It was an issue for Benitez, who liked him as a player and saw enough to hand him the captaincy as a short-term measure after taking over.

Sensing Sissoko could yet be the golden goose, Newcastle let it be known that it would take £35m to prise him from them. The midfielder was astounded. His worried agents contacted the club, insisting there was genuine interest in him from – among others – Bayern Munich, Real Madrid and Juventus. It had the sound of a threat but Benitez was unmoved. "We are not a stepping stone," he'd insisted earlier that summer. "We are Newcastle United."

Sissoko was about to find out Benitez's intransigence was matched by Charnley's desire to extract the best price he could.

If there was one thing Newcastle had done well under his charge, it was to 'sell well'. Sissoko's agent was told that speaking in public was only stiffening the club's resolve not to sell him on the cheap.

***

BENITEZ'S new model army trained twice a day for the first four weeks of summer. There were double sessions, the manager always on the training field – stopping, instructing, cajoling. The system was king. Benitez wanted his players to know it inside out. There was a snap about the way they trained: hunger was back.

It was here that Benitez drilled the players about the system. A defensive unit was constructed – the centre-backs and full-backs put in long hours. His plan was communicated and repeated. Benitez told his players that, to get the winning mentality back, they would have to take it on to the training ground every day. That meant not a single session could be approached without a professional, winning mindset.

"When I was a young player, I hated losing. As you get older, you understand it happens. You have to manage it. Losing is part of the game but you have to retain a winning mentality," he says. "You can say that you have it, but it is not just about that. You have to be sure that every time you go out, you try to win. You try to do your best every time – that is a winning mentality."

The friendlies arrived quickly. They were announced quickly, without fuss. Pre-season had been a problem in the past. Two farcical tales stick in the mind. United had baked in Orlando in 2011, players peeled off the floor in a heat wave that saw an elderly patron staying at their hotel die before their arrival.

The mercury rose and so did the faint whiff of chaos. A game against Orlando City, a third-tier side, was nearly cancelled the night before Newcastle arrived because their synthetic pitch was not what they had described in the brochure. Hasty improvements were made, but still Newcastle were forced into resting key players rather than risk joint injuries.

That was a summer that ended with Joey Barton tweeting his discontent from the back of a bus in Leeds, after vocally expressing his irritation at being whipped from dead-ball duties in a pre-season friendly at Elland Road.

The second, in 2012, saw the club forced into arranging two games on the German border – scrambling to confirm them with a few hours' notice. That was because a mooted trip to Durban to take part in the Vodacom Challenge with a seven-figure entry fee fell through. Commercial considerations over sporting ones.

Benitez took control. He pared-back the arrangements. The furthest they would travel would be to Belgium for a whistle-stop trip to play Sporting Lokeren. Southend, Dublin, Doncaster – Newcastle's opponents were hand-picked to represent the styles of the clubs they would meet in the early weeks of the season.

Things felt efficient. His management style was inspiring some unlikely improvements: Yoan Gouffran, a symbol of McClaren's mediocrity when called to staff the midfield at Manchester City in the Premier League relegation season, had caught Benitez's eye. At initial meetings with the players in pre-season, he had told them that anyone could force their way into his thinking. It was up to them. Gouffran was not part of the original plans and had been told he could leave. But his work was good. He fitted into the system. When he scored a spectacular goal at Southend, he further earned Benitez's trust. Gouffran may not have been the star name, but Benitez's priority was to "balance" his team. That meant the best players for his system, and – especially away from home – he liked Gouffran and Matt Ritchie on either side.

The Rafalution narrative had taken off among Newcastle's support. Excitement was building for their first assignment at Craven Cottage: a tough opener against an unpredictable Fulham side.

***

STEVE McCLAREN was back. The sporting summer was over and Newcastle were about to start a new season. He wore the same smile; the same smart black suit. Before the game, he strolled on to the pitch, shaking hands with some of the players and stopping for a short chat. For those tuning in to Sky Sports and those thronging the stands at Fulham's historic ground, it would have been enough to bring them out in a cold sweat.

It was a hot day at one of English football's most evocative stages. Located on the banks of the River Thames, the walk to Fulham's ground is a pleasant summer's stroll through Bishop's Park – an area gentrified by pop-up cafes, shiny silver burger vans and the unmistakable thump of tennis ball on racket on long sizzling evenings, like the one that greeted Newcastle on the first Friday of the English football season.

For those clad in black and white, the genteel surroundings concealed the hardest of matches. Fulham are hardly London's slickest team but they had triumphed five times in a row at home against Newcastle. There was something about the cramped, claustrophobic atmosphere – the wooden, rickety seats in the main stand a throwback to the days of yore – that seemed to suffocate black and white hopes when they turned up in west London. The appearance of McClaren, drafted in by Sky to provide analysis and expert insight into matters Newcastle, provided an ominous portent for what was to come.

Newcastle had started the game as the shortest-ever Championship favourites. At online bookies Bet365, they moved quickly to shorten Newcastle from 5/1 to 9/4 favourites.

Steve Freeth is paid to assess the markets. Odds of 5/1 was a favourite's shot, but when Benitez agreed to stay money started pouring in. "If Newcastle got a bit of momentum behind them, we felt they were going to be difficult to beat," he explained.

The markets moved even more in the days before Fulham. Still the money kept on coming, to the point that the company was facing its biggest ante-post pay-out if the club actually managed to do it. Forget the Hollywood glamour of a few hardy punters backing Leicester at 5,000/1 – a manageable liability that could be hyped up into a great PR story – this was really big money.

"The Mike Ashley factor was what was preventing us from shortening it before. But when Rafa stayed it sent a message about the direction Newcastle were moving in. The fact the whole club was moving in it together was very appealing to people."

Benitez must have sensed something was off from the start. It took him minutes to jump from the dug-out to urge more responsibility in play from his midfield. He had gone with Jack Colback and Isaac Hayden, a combination that copied his tendency to try and create a midfield shield to protect his 'number ten'. Jonjo Shelvey was kicking his heels on the bench.

It looked wrong and disjointed. It felt like a McClaren performance: washed out and insipid. From the sidelines, it felt natural to worry about the way it all looked. Fulham had finished 20th the season before and had behind-the-scenes worries of their own, but they looked ominously comfortable. Had Benitez prioritised pragmatism at the expense of punch?

Matt Smith, a 6ft 6ins Brummie striker, scored with a header. Newcastle's response was laboured. Benitez called it a "wake-up call". It was a sharp fall from the giddy heights of the summer but, even in defeat, there was something stirring.

In the dressing room, it wasn't quiet or solemn. Players were talking to each other, offering advice and insight into what each of them could do better. Improvement was on the agenda, not recriminations. There was a trust developing among the group.

When their plane landed back in Newcastle airport's private terminal after a short flight, Benitez was pulled to one side and shown a link to an interview with *Foot Mercato* given by Sissoko in France, reaffirming his desire to leave. He talked about Real, his dreams and his wonderful summer with France. After Benitez had spoken to him during the week, assuring him that his situation was in hand, it felt like another unnecessary distraction.

"It was fine returning to Newcastle," Sissoko said. "I had the opportunity to see my colleagues and they were happy with how I did in the Euros. They support me, they were behind me."

Benitez does not normally lose his cool but he was angry. He had promised a club that would have respect for its public but this was a direct challenge to his vision for a Newcastle rowing in the same direction. Whether intended or not – and Sissoko insisted the timing was not his – for the article to emerge shortly after a game in which his team were playing was the height of disrespect. When Benitez was building a team that 'got it', that would have to prepare to act as a team, here was one who steadfastly refused.

Any thoughts of rehabilitation before the transfer window closed – and there had been some when the offers did not come for Sissoko – surely ended that night.

***

NEWCASTLE'S next game was Huddersfield. This was meant to be the warm-up to the harder challenges of September's fixture list. The Terriers had finished the previous season fighting relegation but had attracted some coverage for the way their manager, David Wagner, a former assistant to Jurgen Klopp, had approached the challenge of inspiring the Terriers to outfight the bigger guns of a division loaded with historic rivals.

Newcastle were not the only team in the division with history. Aston Villa had dropped with United, and also had a Champions League-winning boss at the helm: Roberto Di Matteo. Sheffield Wednesday and Leeds regularly jousted for honours in the early '90s before a fall from grace that saw both Yorkshire sides playing in the third tier. Nottingham Forest – another former European Cup winner – were in the same boat, another sunken giant.

For Huddersfield, competing with teams that picked up parachute payments for recent stints in the Premier League, the only way to compete was to match them for spirit. Wagner coined the phrase 'Terrier identity', reasoning they were small but aggressive. "We have fighting spirit, for sure," he said.

They had spent their summer in a spartan Swedish training camp with no electricity. They had to find their own food, start their own fires and make their own way. It had bonded them. They tore out of the blocks.

Newcastle were pressed to death: Nahki Wells scored on the stroke of half-time. A sold-out St James' Park inhaled deeply. Dwight Gayle responded by reacting quickest to a saved penalty. But they were hit with a sucker punch when Jack Payne scored on 82 minutes. Newcastle had not played badly, but the wit and intelligence that had been on view at the end of the previous season seemed to be missing. Shelvey was in midfield now, but it did not make a difference. Newcastle's hungry new team were met by foes who looked more desperate to prove themselves. Huddersfield celebrated as if they had won the FA Cup. As the fans filed out of St James' Park, anxiety mixed with fatalism.

Benitez had earned trust – it would take more than that to shake their belief. No-one was panicking, no-one was heckling. But no points from six was a start that no-one had expected.

This was a test. Previous managers might have blinked. Benitez, undeterred, told his players to keep doing what they were doing. "You'll win if we keep following the plan," he said. They listened.

Having been urged to believe again, the undercurrent of worry was understandable. Newcastle's start in their last promotion season was not without its problems but they had played the 20th and 19th finishers from the previous campaign and not emerged with a point. Was the Rafalution nothing but a mirage?

8. Card Games And Chess

What Shapes The Manager's Football Philosophy

"In Spain we have a card game called 'Mus'. The key is how quickly you can find a solution. I have always been like that"

Rafa Benitez, December 2016

RAFA BENITEZ has always loved games. In the summers that he wasn't playing or watching football – the game that he really loved – he'd fill his hours playing chess or 'Mus', a card game popular in Spain and France.

The rules of 'Mus' sound long-winded but, essentially, boil down to one thing: you are required to gamble on the strength of your hand. The suits are cards, batons, cups and coins and there are eight Reys – or kings – four Caballos (horses), numbered jacks and eight aces. It's a game of bluff, where you have to make quick, snap decisions on the strength of your hand.

Pull a king-king-king-king in the first round and you'll win the hand. But in the second round the same hand is a disaster. Benitez loved the game – and he still does. Long days on the training ground are punctuated by games of Mus between the coaching staff. There is no money involved, just the pride of getting one over 'the boss'.

"My way of thinking has always been to analyse things. I like the strategy for battle. I always loved chess," he said. One summer, at the age of 13, he resolved to find a way to never lose to his brother or friends at a military-themed board game called Stratego.

"It was a game I loved. I was always analysing the tactics of it. You have the flag in the middle and you have to protect it. I love that game and I always loved the tactics," he says.

But his older brother was better than him. In his 2012 book, *Champions League Dreams*, he recounts the tale in more detail. 'I have always hated to lose so that summer I tried to work out a way that he would never beat me again.

'So, for one day and one night, I analysed the game, considering each piece, its strengths and weaknesses, how it could best be used. I wrote everything down and drew up a plan.

'I decided how I would play the game, what my strategy would be, and resolved to stick to it. I knew how I would move my pieces, where I would station each part of my army, the attacks that I would make.

'The basic principle was to toy with what my opponent expected me to do, to move the pieces in such a way that they would mistakenly assume certain characters in certain places, and to keep some pieces back, so that you did not risk losing by finding your forces suddenly depleted.

'All of my work did not go to waste. My brother and my friends would never beat me again.'

Decades later, he found himself in Istanbul, Turkey, his dreams of winning the Champions League in tatters after a ruinous first half with Liverpool 3-0 down having been totally out-played by AC Milan. There was no convention for what to do next. Jamie Carragher spoke of the need to restore pride or keep the score down. In the dressing room that night Benitez got to work, employing the same logic that had inspired him in that frantic 24 hours in his childhood.

To a man obsessed with winning, it must have felt like the realisation of a nightmare. Benitez must have been feeling the same emotion that Carragher described: embarrassment. The fulfilment of a dream, the pride at walking out for a game that would be the pinnacle of your football career – all destroyed by a 45-minute Milanese masterclass. But if he was in trouble, he wasn't showing it.

'My admiration for his handling of the situation is unlimited. Rafa's conduct rarely changed, regardless of the circumstances. His calm demeanour was never required more than now,' Carragher wrote in his autobiography.

Andrea Pirlo was dictating play in the centre of midfield. So Benitez switched to 3-5-2, removing Steve Finnan and replacing him with Dietmar Hamann. He would have Steven Gerrard and Hamann outnumbering the maestro in midfield. Djibril Cisse came on at right midfield for Djimi Traore.

The manager's command of English was still rudimentary but the speed-of-thought provided the clarity that the dressing room needed. The rest – the comeback, the win, Benitez's tactical acumen – is now part of Anfield folklore. If he could do that, should there ever have been a doubt that he could manoeuvre a way out of Newcastle's desperate start?

Around Christmas, Benitez quietly mentioned to one of Newcastle's media staff that the 2-0 win at Wigan was his 1,000th game in football. It was an understated moment but the event allowed him to come off the beaten path of the Championship promotion chase and contemplate his career to date.

"In football it is the same (as Stratego). You have a plan A, a plan B. Sometimes that doesn't work so you have to go to plan C," he said.

Reading were next-up, at St James' Park. Benitez was already working on the solution.

***

TO get to the heart of Rafa Benitez's football philosophy, you have to realise that it has been pieced together since he was 13. Then he was a young holding midfielder who liked to sit as deep as possible on the pitch, so he could take in everything that was going on. His ruminations were broken by just one thing: the shrill sound of his father's whistling.

"My father, when I played, was always whistling at me from the sidelines. That meant, 'Stop talking and try to get the ball in the net.' That was what he was telling me because I was a holding midfielder telling my teammates: 'Go here, go there'. I like to manage. I like to look from the outside because I have this vision.

"As a player I was never top class. I could be a player in a mid-table team because I was very professional, I liked to train and was very focused. But I was not at the level of a top side. I tried to compensate with my understanding. I was better playing deeper so I could see more of the pitch. That's why I was a sweeper at university. I always liked tactics. When I was 13 I had my notebook with all of the points for the players I was playing with, and all of my notes on the tactics."

Back home on the Wirral, he still has the notebook. One day, he may go back to it. There could be a lesson from the Real Madrid under-14 side of the 1973/74 season that remains relevant well over 40 years later.

It was often said during Newcastle's 2016/17 season that no manager since Sir Bobby Robson had been as well-qualified for the position – and experience was one of Benitez's greatest weapons in the Championship promotion race. Peter Schmeichel had posted a message on social media shortly after Benitez's appointment questioning why Newcastle hadn't gone for a motivator like Nigel Pearson to take the job on a short-term basis.

There were similar questions about Benitez's lack of experience of Championship football. "People were saying from the start, Benitez doesn't know the Championship," he said after promotion had been won. His belief was that, whatever the level, whoever the players, football is about finding solutions: about adapting, flexibility, questioning what is going on around you and plotting a path to victory.

It meant being pragmatic, too. When Jonjo Shelvey got into full flow and Matt Ritchie started hammering defenders in between the lines, Newcastle could be easy on the eye. But they were also dogged: ruthlessly and relentlessly so at times. Benitez's Newcastle followed in a black and white tradition by playing with width and enterprise, but they also went direct. Benitez was unashamed about the need to be flexible, especially when he had a player in Shelvey who could hit long passes so effectively. Sometimes, the problems required more prosaic solutions.

Benitez learned from Stratego to "keep some pieces back" so that you did not risk losing your flag by exposing your depleted forces to the enemy. Newcastle would be built from the back. The solution to be solved from the first two games was to eradicate the defensive errors that had handed Fulham and Huddersfield Town their easy goals.

***

WHEN Rafa Benitez was 26, he took charge of the Real Madrid

Castilla B side. It was his first game in management. Nervous, tense, he named a squad of 15 because the club told him that he could only have four substitutes, not five as he had presumed. Real lost 2-1. He was infuriated to see that their opponents had named five players on the bench. It ate away at him for weeks.

'That defeat taught me an important lesson. Fine details matter. Who knows, that extra substitute could have made all the difference,' he wrote in *Champions League Dreams*. Take care of everything, leave nothing to chance.

There were Champions League winners at other clubs in the Championship that season – including another who had won the biggest prize in football more recently than Benitez. But did Aston Villa's Roberto Di Matteo have the hunger Benitez possessed?

Back on the training ground he got to work. Two defeats might have shaken the city but there was an assurance about Benitez's manner that felt like the polar opposite of panic. Subtle tweaks were required but the direction remained the same. Benitez was convinced that it was the way to win. It may not have been the elite environment he had been used to at Real, Napoli or Liverpool, but he went about his work in the Championship with the zeal of a rookie manager.

He was the first person in, the last out. His family were a few hours away on the Wirral. During his days at Liverpool, he would sometimes take his work home with him. At Newcastle, he stayed in his training ground office until late. There was a match on virtually every night that he wanted to watch, so it made more sense to him to view it in the company of his own coaches, rather than in his rented house. "We didn't want to waste too much time," he says, explaining the work ethic that drove the staff during the course of the season.

***

A MIDWEEK, match night in Newcastle. Wednesday night lights: the return of competitive football to the working week in a city where the game – whoever Newcastle are playing – always feels a little bit more special. This season, the midweek Championship fixtures would come thick and fast: a total of 14 in a season that was super-sized from the Premier League programme.

Benitez told the players the team. Again, he had made big changes to the starting XI. Captain Jamaal Lascelles was left out. Rolando Aarons, the speedy winger brought through the Academy, was also absent.

Yoan Gouffran, the player whose presence led to a teamsheet double take at the Etihad the season before, came in from the cold to play on the left of midfield. With teams from France ready to take him back over the Channel, there was the prospect that this would be his final game. Given the feeling among supporters after the announcement that night, there may not have been too many tears if he was sold and replaced.

For those who saw Benitez's teamsheets in isolation, the dropping of Lascelles – a new captain, selected for the certainty of his opinions the previous season – felt like a message to the defender. He had been poor at Fulham and the defence had been porous at home to Huddersfield. To the untrained eye, it had the feel of a manager asserting his authority.

Perhaps in a dressing room used to certain players being fixtures, it might have had that feel to it. Moussa Sissoko was still on the books – exiled, of course – but many had felt that he was undroppable when he was in the first-team reckoning, even though it sometimes felt like he turned in two lethargic performances for every undoubted match-turning display.

Lascelles took the decision well – and so he should have done. Benitez's rotation policy was not a power play or an act of punishment, even if it was a Tyneside obsession during those early months of the season.

Instead, it came from an index that Benitez updated daily. After every match and every training session, either the manager or one of his coaching staff would take notes on observations about how the players were performing. Was one of them tired? Did one seem to be struggling with a turn of pace? Had one reacted better to a situation put in front of him than expected?

On his desk at Darsley Park, there were stacks of neatly piled pieces of paper with blue, green and red boxes. Players names, phrases in English and percentages next to them. It is here where the team selections are decided.

In the autumn, having not played the same team consecutively all season, Benitez explained what was going on. "People need to be reassured that we have a lot of information, we see the players in training. For example, Yedlin had problems in his ankles after tackles in the previous two games. We also have Anita, who is playing and training well, so why not play him instead and give Yedlin a rest?

"We have a lot of information and we try to manage this to put the strongest team on the pitch. We're not improvising.

"We also have our software – after every game you will see me taking notes, well it goes into the software. It's about the strengths and weaknesses of the team in those games and we can return to it after 10 games and revisit it.

"We start working on that. Paco [Francisco De Miguel Moreno] has been working for years with me and he reviews it after a set period. After maybe 10 games he will say, 'We need to improve the counter attack', so we put on more sessions on that.

"But we don't change after every game, we work in the longer term. The idea is that little-by-little we are improving things as we go along. We have a plan which we follow."

It was the strongest team on the available information to hand. Nothing to chance. No stone left unturned.

On the first Wednesday of the season, it was enough. Jaap

Stam's Reading were, similarly, a work in progress – another fascinating Championship sub-plot in a season packed with them. He'd recruited a squad on a budget with an intention to turn them into a possession-based side and, over the course of the season, it certainly worked. Newcastle had to find a solution.

They started well and were ahead through Isaac Hayden, a lively performer stoking the fires in the engine room. Newcastle's industry was causing problems but, as the half wore on, Reading grew into the game.

In each of their previous two matches, Newcastle had conceded on 45 minutes. The crowd knew that and the atmosphere grew edgy. Reading advanced; Ciaran Clark's untidy lunge upended the mobile John Swift in the penalty area. Garath McCleary swept home the penalty to level the match. Newcastle had another problem to solve.

At half-time, Benitez remained serene. The message to his players was about consistency. His desired system was to keep Dwight Gayle up front, breaking into channels and working the opposition back four while Ayoze Perez offered balance behind him. Ritchie was also central.

Reading cracked in the second half, conceded a penalty of their own that Ritchie dispatched. Then came Gayle's double: his first, a wonderful 30-yard free-kick that was met with relief around St James' Park. Newcastle were up and running.

"Tonight was about the result," Benitez said afterwards. The character had impressed him. Newcastle were no more than a seven out of 10 that night – a point picked up by Stam, who complained that his team had been the better side at St James' Park. "We were the better team but they've won and we've got nothing," he said.

There were signs that it was coming together. Nobody needed to be told that Newcastle would have to move through the gears to assert themselves on the Championship.

"We can play much better than that. We will improve," Benitez said. He was building a team and a mentality, step by step, minute-by-minute.

***

ON the training ground, things grew sharper. The threat of rotation kept players on their toes: the knowledge that it was not personal or a decision taken on a whim meant that insecurities were managed.

Benitez's man-management techniques had been questioned by his former charge Steven Gerrard but at Newcastle, players noted the warmth of the man who had been painted as cold by others. In Madrid, news leaked of Cristiano Ronaldo becoming irked when Benitez emailed him a bespoke video detailing ways to shake off his marker. However, Newcastle players did not mind the interventions.

"He is very approachable when you've been left out of the team," Shelvey said. "You can knock on his door and ask for advice and he will give it to you."

It had been the same in the summer: little moments, even among players who were injured. On the day they cut Rob Elliot's thigh tendon off, the goalkeeper was just coming around from the anesthetic when a text from Benitez popped up on his phone.

"'Hi Rob, hope the injury is well.' He then asked me which players I liked for the Championship. I thought I might put Keegan," Elliot told *The Irish Times*. "I thought, 'Wow, he's staying and he wants my opinion. It was a massive lift.'"

Benitez liked Elliot's character: he had noticed the way the other players looked up to him. Quietly, and without fuss, he offered Elliot a long-term contract when he was out injured, which the goalkeeper signed.

These subtle tweaks were helping to change the mentality of the group. It felt more of a collective. The individualism of the previous group was evaporating. Newcastle had a team again and, even when you lost your place, the important thing was that the side was getting better, stronger. All of the players knew that if they continued to perform to their maximum, it would be difficult for Benitez to find a reason to rotate them.

Then came a milestone. Few Newcastle fans would single out Ashton Gate or August 20 as significant to Benitez's attempts to transform the club, but they were the culmination of months of work trying to solve an inability to win away from home.

It was a serious deficiency to Benitez. Playing away from St James' Park revealed character. It required discipline and mettle. It ate away at the Spaniard that the team had not had either the character, nor the characters to win on their travels in the Premier League and he believed that this group would be able to solve that issue.

At Craven Cottage familiar problems of shape and personality had re-emerged. If the team failed to find a formula on the road, Benitez knew they would come up short. He drew up a plan that was to have a huge restorative effect on their form away from Tyneside.

"The away form was one of the things I had to find a solution for," he says. He told the players that they had technical ability but it would not be enough on its own to win games at stadiums where their arrival would herald the biggest afternoon of the season for the home side. Tenacity – not technique – was his mantra.

"If you want to improve anything you need to have the right attitude," he said.

"In modern football we talk too much about quality, but what is quality? It's not just to stop the ball and put it 40 metres or score a brilliant free-kick, that is technical ability.

"Quality is about doing the right things. To win games you need both effort and attitude."

They went to Bristol City having not picked up an away win since December, but won 1-0. Gayle scored the winning goal, a brilliantly instinctive strike. The home side battered Newcastle in the closing stages, urged on by a capacity crowd. United held firm. The message was getting through: to the players, supporters and the rest of the Championship. Newcastle United were no longer a soft touch.

9. The Leadership Problem

Turning Up The Volume In A Squad Full Of Quiet Men

"Everyone has a plan until they're hit in the mouth"

Mike Tyson, 1988

MATT RITCHIE applied just the right amount of venom to his left-wing free-kick to inject panic in the Brighton penalty area. Given the opposition, that was no mean feat. Chris Hughton's team would go on to establish themselves as the best defensive unit in the Championship – expertly marshalled by Lewis Dunk, in the heart of their back four, a player of England potential that Newcastle have tried to sign on numerous occasions.

David Stockdale, the goalkeeper, has an air of authority that radiates through the back four. The previous season, Brighton were pipped to the second automatic promotion spot by Middlesbrough on the final day. Their manager looked at Boro's 31 goals conceded and identified it as the hurdle his side would have to surmount to go one better, in a league that now had Newcastle as unwanted squatters in the promotion race. Over the course of the season, that back four would provide the backbone for so many gritty wins. When they travelled north, they had only conceded two goals from four games. Three clean sheets: a pattern had been set.

But on the fourth week of the Championship season, Rafa Benitez found a solution. Ritchie's free-kick was met by Jamaal Lascelles with a ferocious header. Brighton's resistance was broken on 15 minutes. The visitors were rattled, reduced to 10 men shortly after the start of the second half. Dwight Gayle was injured so Jonjo Shelvey stepped up to take a 63rd-minute free-kick that dipped past Stockdale.

Five games in, three league wins on the spin after the opening defeats. Up to fourth. Newcastle were up and running. So, too, was the newly-crowned captain.

***

In his book *Legacy* about the all-conquering New Zealand All Blacks, James Kerr devotes a fascinating chapter to the leadership culture that fires the most successful sporting team in the world.

It's called 'Responsibility' and details how the All Blacks do things differently. They don't run on to the pitch with a rousing team talk ringing in their ears. By that point, coach Graham Henry explains, the work has been done over the days and weeks leading up to the Test Match. And although the instructions and strategy come from the top, the culture of New Zealand's rugby union team is to devolve responsibility for leadership to the group. 'The management also felt that they had to transfer the leadership from senior management members to the players. The traditional "you and them" became "us".'

It was not an overnight transition. They gradually devolved responsibility to the players.

Steve McClaren had read *Legacy*. His friend Steve Black, the so-called 'mind mechanic' who had worked with Jonny Wilkinson to hone the World Cup-winning fly-half's mental strength, wanted to create a similar culture at Newcastle. But they were hampered by the group that they inherited. The mix was not right. "Passive," McClaren called it later. "Very quiet."

When they went behind in games, there was rarely any coming back. Twice, McClaren felt he'd cracked it. Steven Taylor led a fabulous rearguard action alongside Chancel Mbemba in the heart of the defence at Old Trafford in the early weeks of the 2015/16 season, keeping a clean sheet against Manchester United. Then at Bournemouth, a heroic Rob Elliot helped Newcastle to cling on for a 1-0 victory. "I felt we were on the cusp of developing," the goalkeeper later said.

"We lost to Watford in January, who were big and strong. Maybe we didn't have the character to stand up to that. If it was just a football game, we could hold our own because we had good, technical players."

Around the dressing room, Newcastle looked for leaders in their darkest hours during the relegation season but there were none to be found. Coloccini, disenchanted, struggling for his own form, did not possess it. Moussa Sissoko was a big noise, but as concerned with his own game as he was with that of others. Georginio Wijnaldum possessed some of the famous Dutch bravado but he was new to the country. He quickly recognised that he was, perhaps, destined for only a short stay on Tyneside and his attitude recalibrated accordingly.

Lascelles was not an obvious source to inject some of that leadership into Newcastle's ailing group. He had just returned from

Nottingham Forest in the Championship, where he'd spent a year on loan. Big, athletic, brave and quick, he had all the attributes to be an England defender but there were flaws in his game that opponents knew about. McClaren did not consider him ready for the Premier League.

Lascelles waited but grew frustrated at what he saw around him. He bit his tongue but, when he got into the team, he couldn't hold back much longer. The swearing against Everton – "Nobody gives a f***" – after being sent off in a 3-0 defeat at Goodison Park was the catalyst.

"Partly it was frustration at myself. We needed big characters and I felt a lot of ours weren't putting a shift in. That's why I said it. There were a few arguments afterwards," he said.

His team-mates came back at him. They questioned him: a few asked who he thought he was to speak to them like that. Lascelles came back at them again, accusing them of letting down the manager. "The conflict was good. It was exactly what we needed," McClaren reasoned.

Benitez's goal at the club was to create a management group that would solve the problems identified by McClaren, John Carver and Alan Pardew.

Newcastle had one once, led by Kevin Nolan. The players' committee distributed the fines, drew up the media list and the dressing room policed itself. Hughton – the Newcastle manager in those days – had signed his own death warrant with the suspicious United board by letting it grow. They felt it was hot housing mutiny and, when a bonus schedule that was supposed to be signed before the start of the Premier League season in 2011 was the subject of a player rebellion, Hughton and the idea of a strong dressing room were abandoned. Had they been allowed to flourish, things might have been different. But the hierarchy had it disbanded in a power play that was one of the most damaging things done in the Mike Ashley era.

Benitez had a different way of doing things. He had signed players with character and charisma. There were several in his group who he considered for the armband, but the most important thing was that they started to take responsibility for changing the direction of matches again.

That famous Mike Tyson quote: "Everyone has a plan until they get punched in the mouth", felt particularly relevant at Newcastle. Their response to adversity had been found wanting over the years – Benitez knew that could not be the case in a long, testing Championship season. Inevitably, tensions would arise, nerves would become frayed. Resilience was going to be important.

Benitez's nature is to be obsessive. He is over everything but he is not a control freak, as some other managers are. On the touchline he will cajole, urge and instruct his players at different points of the game. When he first arrived at Newcastle, it looked like he was walking the players through the games, such was his frenzied desire to communicate his message from the touchline. But that was not a long-term strategy for changing Newcastle's leadership dynamic.

Lascelles was to be the figurehead, handed the armband by virtue of his bravery in talking out to more senior players. Benitez figured that giving the job to a player who was young would also open the floor to others, who had felt too cowed by the experienced – or more talented – foreign imports to speak out.

The pride in Lascelles' voice when he talked about the honour was genuine. He visited community events and spoke to the media. That was important. Coloccini had taken criticism for refusing to front up: the player himself insisted it was because his poor command of English meant that he felt he could not get his message across clearly.

Benitez's Newcastle, like the All Blacks, did not leave the pitch to rousing, Churchillian speeches from their manager. The minutes before the game were used to offer instructions but the work had been done in the weeks or days before. The cross words of McClaren at Everton were never exchanged in the dressing room in the Championship season, even if the players themselves were prepared to challenge each other.

Lascelles was the team's figurehead. The players' response to adversity changed under Benitez. Many more were prepared to challenge their own performances – privately and publicly. Mo Diame admitted that his performances weren't good enough at Christmas. Shelvey said the same in the early weeks of the season. Lascelles fronted up about letting his own levels drop.

At Fulham on the opening day, Benitez stayed quiet in the corner, listening to the players direct constructive criticism at each other. Often they spoke of the importance of their responsibilities as Newcastle players – to the club, to the supporters who had invested their faith in the group. The dynamic was shifting.

***

BEFORE they played again, there was unfinished business to attend to. The end of the summer transfer window coincided with the first week of an international break and Moussa Sissoko's future remained uncertain.

Benitez had made Sissoko captain when he first arrived at Newcastle: a pragmatic move to squeeze the best from him and also from a group that recognised the midfielder's importance when they were playing well. Privately, he said that the French-speaking players in the squad saw him as their talisman. A short-term fix was to get Sissoko revved up again.

The pair got on well. The players might have been portrayed as arrogant and aloof at certain points during their relegation season but the dynamic was a bit more complicated. When they gathered in the canteen before meeting Benitez for the first time, the chatter was that of excited school kids meeting someone famous.

Benitez used that influence to his advantage with players like Sissoko, who felt they had outgrown the club.

Old school British managers might have described it as a 'medals on the table' moment. Sir Bobby Robson certainly had no qualms in using his experience at some of the world's top clubs to curb the confidence of his so-called 'Brat pack' of talented Newcastle players. Benitez was a bit more subtle than that, but he knew it was a good way to knock the edges off a group who had let his predecessor down.

At first he thought that might extend into the Championship year. Sissoko, on form, would have been the best player in the division and he was told that he would not have to sell him.

But it soon became apparent that, of all the players who wanted to leave the club, none was as resolute and determined as Sissoko was to depart.

Benitez had wanted to keep Andros Townsend and the pair's relationship was strong enough to make the winger seriously consider taking a step into the Championship. At Newcastle, Townsend had finally found somewhere he belonged. Benitez loved Townsend's work ethic and willingness to listen and grow. Twice he asked him to stay. Townsend was close to agreeing – until Crystal Palace offered him the chance to remain in the Premier League. He respected his wish to leave to further an international career that would have stalled in the second tier.

Similarly, Benitez liked Florian Thauvin. He had tried to sign him at Inter Milan and Napoli and would have welcomed the chance to work with him. But Thauvin's head had never been in Newcastle from the moment he signed a contract that was – in his words – "too good to turn down". He didn't want to go to Newcastle, had turned the club down twice and didn't like the cold, the food or the style of play in England. At Watford, in the FA Cup, he was booed by his own supporters and used that as a bargaining chip with the hierarchy to negotiate a loan move out of the club. Benitez offered him a way back but Thauvin wanted to return to France. Nonetheless, he trained well while he waited for the move. Benitez had respect for that.

Sissoko was different. He was a good family man who enjoyed English football: the cut and thrust of the Premier League. But he was also a clothes horse with aspirations of being the best midfielder in Europe with an ego to match his ambitions. Successive managers recognised his talent and at Euro 2016, France's footballing coming home party, he excelled. He was Man of the Match in the final against Portugal and there was no way back for him from there.

But the window dragged on and no-one would pay the £30m that Newcastle wanted. Benitez would have known that rehabilitating him if he'd stayed would have been difficult but he approved of Lee Charnley's high stakes game.

On deadline day – finally – Everton bit. Newcastle had turned down an £18m offer from Tottenham earlier in the transfer window, insistent that they would only accept their original, post-Euro valuation.

New Everton boss Ronald Koeman really wanted him. His board sanctioned the bid and Sissoko left the France training camp in Clairefontaine, ready to move to Goodison Park. A deal was in the offing but Sissoko's heart was set on the Champions League, and Spurs were the only team that had qualified for the competition who were showing an interest. Koeman telephoned Sissoko to welcome him to the club but the midfielder wouldn't answer his calls. The private jet that was chartered for Sissoko was never boarded.

Tottenham moved in. A deal that would see the club pay five instalments of £6m was agreed. Sissoko, who had stayed in London, made the short trip to sign the deal.

Benitez saw it as a huge success. Newcastle had ended the transfer window with a huge net profit: offering him leeway with anyone who would accuse the club of buying the league. It should also mean money to spend for January. It was MD Lee Charnley's greatest success of the transfer window.

More importantly, it paved the way for that shifting dressing room dynamic to continue without the distraction of an unsettled player still being at the club.

Cheick Tiote, still desperate to leave but without an interested buyer, did remain though. But he could be easily managed on his own. Everyone else in the dressing room saw Newcastle as the destination rather than the platform. That shift in collective attitude was going to play a massive part in Benitez's continued rebuilding process.

***

NEWCASTLE'S ability to respond when punched in the mouth remained – largely, thankfully – untested for the next few weeks. They returned from the international break to beat struggling Derby County 2-0 and then on a crazy, cathartic night in West London they thrashed Queens Park Rangers 6-0, with Shelvey scoring a wonderful, swirling shot that was the best goal of the Magpies' season.

Then they lost to Wolverhampton Wanderers at St James' Park, a 2-0 defeat that was to have to ramifications further down the line. It was avenged in the EFL Cup against the same opponents in midweek but Newcastle were then left frustrated by a 1-1 draw with Aston Villa at Villa Park, when they failed to put the home side to the sword.

They sat fifth in the Championship. Goalkeeper Matz Sels, who was having an unexpectedly brittle introduction to life in England, deleted his Twitter account after receiving criticism from some fans on the social media site. Benitez recognised the twitchiness. On the training ground, the same, consistent message was delivered. He had faith in the group. Norwich City, second in the table and starting to look ominously impressive, were next up at St James' Park.

10. Dwight Gayle Rides The Bus

How Key Man Took The Road Less Travelled

"He was a skinny little kid but he had the heart of a lion"

Dave Bricknell, 2016

BISHOP'S STORTFORD were in trouble. Deep, deep trouble.

The football club under the flight path of Stansted had crash-landed in English football's equivalent of purgatory. A club that plays its home games in a pretty market town near Essex had been transferred into the Conference North for season 2011/12, the sixth tier of English football and home to the likes of Colwyn Bay, Harrogate Town, Workington and Blyth Spartans.

At this level, you count the pennies, never mind the pounds. The club was left incredulous. The locations of the three teams relegated from the Conference – plus the demise of Rushden & Diamonds – meant an imbalance in the Conference North and South divisions. The Blues, being the northernmost club in the oversubscribed South for 2011/12, were duly placed in the North division, a decision which would mean that every single away game would see them criss-cross the country before the match had even begun, not to mention the financial implications.

They had former England goalkeeper Ian Walker in charge. He'd been appointed with the big idea of moving the club up a level but the sales pitch quickly turned into: do you really fancy it? Nobody in their right mind would. At this level, most of the players are semi-professional. You pick up decent money but the payoff is that you have to balance training and playing commitments with a career elsewhere. Now the Blues had to break it to their squad that every other week they'd be catching a bus at 2am on a Saturday morning. It wasn't the kind of environment that Walker – who wanted to follow in the footsteps of his father Mike into management – was accustomed to.

Some players left. The ones Walker tried to sign were having second thoughts. When they were offered the chance to take a skinny striker who had been playing Essex League Football, they didn't really have much choice.

Enter Dwight Gayle. Five years before he wore Newcastle's number nine shirt, he was sitting at the back of the bus on the way to Harrogate.

It was the year Newcastle finished fifth in the Premier League. They'd just spent £10m on Papiss Cisse from Freiburg. Gayle was earning £150 a week, having taken a pay cut to join John Still's Dagenham & Redbridge, taking the opportunity to have one last shot at a professional football career.

***

DWIGHT GAYLE RIDES THE BUS

RIDGEWAY ROVERS' training pitches used to be situated next to the old Walthamstow Greyhound Stadium in Chingford. Given he was whippet-quick but as wiry as a rake, it seemed like an appropriate place for Gayle to make his formative steps into football. Gayle was five when Dave Bricknell, a coach at Ridgeway, first saw him kick a ball. It was 1995, the year after David Beckham – one of Bricknell's former charges – had made an eye-catching debut for Manchester United. His phone had already started to ring: journalists eager to know more about the route Beckham had taken to Old Trafford.

Harry Kane also passed through those doors. Over the years he got used to the calls, he started getting a bit fed up of them, truth be told. But Bricknell always has time to talk about Gayle, whose story does not follow the same gilded path that Kane – always groomed for greatness at Tottenham – or Beckham's did.

"He was five when I first saw him play and, even then, he was phenomenal for his age. He was quick but it was his movement that was so impressive for a boy of his age. He knew where to go, he knew the moves to make. That made him seem even quicker, because no-one knew where he was going to go so he always had that first couple of yards on his marker," Bricknell recalls.

One year he played in a tournament in the Netherlands and Ridgeway took a game to penalties. Gayle had to take two – and did so with either foot. One year, he scored more than 100 goals – most of them using his explosive pace to peel off the shoulder of the final defender and then finish with either foot. Arsenal scouts had seen him and invited him to their Academy. He seemed like a natural fit but there was a problem. Everyone had noticed.

"He was so small. His frame was small and he was skinny as well. It makes it very difficult for someone like him when the other boys are twice his size," Bricknell remembers.

Arsenal let him go at 13. He returned to Ridgeway and played for fun again. Bricknell couldn't believe it.

"He was skinny but he had the heart of a lion. His leap was incredible. For a small lad, he could jump and he was good in the air but, at those academies, the margin for error is very small. They obviously thought they couldn't take a chance," he says.

His dad, Devon, was 6ft 4ins tall and played for the same Saturday and Sunday league teams that Dwight appeared destined to feature for. There is money turning out for them but not enough to sustain a living. He turned to carpentry and took his exams, passing them all. He combined that with playing and training every night. He was a regular in the gym, working to build his upper-body strength. Bricknell advised Stansted FC to take a look at him. In the ninth tier of English football, he got a foothold back in the game and started scoring again.

Still's scouts were watching. Dagenham & Redbridge were Football League but on a budget. The contract was less than he was earning from carpentry, but there was no question.

"I think there was always a bit of a buzz about him but people aren't always willing to take a chance on talent at that level, especially not in an area where there are so many clubs and it's generally assumed that the best players are already with clubs," Still remembers.

"People aren't prepared to look at non-league anymore but when they come out of an academy and get a second chance they're hungry. You can see that with Dwight: he's got hunger. We tapped into that.

"It was a weird situation because I knew his Dad really well but Dwight didn't know that when I met him. You couldn't miss Devon, he was completely different from Dwight as a player but they shared one thing in common: they could both score goals."

***

GAYLE was taking the route less travelled to the top but the loan to Bishop's Stortford was something else. Sent across Essex to get games, he found himself going north – and carrying a team while he was at it.

Walker left, disillusioned. Rod Stringer took over. Gayle played on the right wing for some of that season and, at first, the step up from Essex League to Conference North looked like it might be the end of the road. Experienced defenders thought they could bully him into submission.

But his head never dropped. If he was asked to do something, he did it. He may have been on a professional contract, but he mucked in with the rest of the team. No-one at the club has a bad word to say about him: every single one loved the way that he embraced the challenge of proving himself.

After Christmas, the hard work paid off. He began to roll off the defenders who had pushed him, his improved upper body strength giving him the edge. That pace became an unstoppable weapon. Bishop's Stortford had started the season preparing for a relegation battle but ended it 10th. Gayle's 45 goals, including a hat-trick on the final day of the season against Eastwood Town in April, were a big reason for it.

He went back to Dagenham and it clicked. The steep upward trajectory continued: now he was worth £450,000 and Championship strugglers Peterborough moved quickly to sign him, negotiating a deal that prompted Still to resign in protest. He was now at the club of Barry Fry, who purred when he saw him in training. "He was the most natural finisher I have ever seen – right foot, left foot, good in the air, he's got the lot," Fry says. "We got relegated and he got 13 goals."

Back in League One, Peterborough had to sell when Crystal Palace came in for him. Then manager Ian Holloway told his chairman "not to leave the room" without him signing for Palace. "The way he moved, I loved it," Holloway said later. "The top strikers make it look easy and he's just got it."

Alan Pardew likened him to Ian Wright but injuries stalled his progress. Palace started to play a different way under Pardew, who liked a big target man for his midfield to play off. That was not Gayle, and frustration grew. Bricknell remembers feeling as frustrated as the striker did.

"We just thought: 'Give him a run of games, he'll score goals'," he said. That was exactly what Rafa Benitez wanted to do.

***

A FEE of £10m is a lot of money. Palace had paid £6m and wanted nearly double when Newcastle enquired. Benitez was prepared to pay it. Gayle's worth was inflating but so, too, were the sizes of the challenge.

Palace had been Premier League and this was the Championship, but Gayle was no longer the young hopeful. Benitez had invested in a player to score goals and ease the burden on the rest of a squad who were among the division's lowest scorers the previous season. Newcastle – the home of Alan Shearer, Jackie Milburn, Malcolm Macdonald – had not had a striker score more than 20 goals for 12 years. That was Shearer, and a lot had happened in the intervening period.

Gayle impressed with his attitude from the off. Benitez appreciated not only the willingness to move down a division, but also his desire to learn. He was not going to be involved in much of the build-up play given the way Benitez wanted him to operate, so his concentration was going to have to improve. When the chance arose, he needed to be first among equals. There could be no hesitation in his head or his boots.

He also wanted Newcastle's number nine shirt, vacated by Cisse. In Newcastle's last Championship season, Chris Hughton had opted not to hand the number nine to young striker Andy Carroll because he felt the pressure and expectation may be too much for him. Gayle was 25 now and ready to be the main man. He wanted the number – and the questions and the pressure that might come with it.

Laudably, Aleksandar Mitrovic, who wore 45 because the two numbers combined to make nine, opted not to take up Benitez's offer of a finishing contest to determine who should have it. "I thought it might make a problem between players," he reasoned, later. Bricknell was overjoyed. "The history of that shirt – you know about it even if you're a Spurs fan, like me. It was a big pressure but I knew Dwight would be able to handle it," he said.

***

WHEN you know how Gayle arrived, his remarkable performance on September 28 – when Newcastle had been punched in the mouth by Norwich – becomes more understandable.

To recall: Newcastle had begun superbly against Norwich. Gayle should have scored before his 24th-minute opener, which was a smart finish from Matt Ritchie's fizzing right-wing cross. Michael McGovern's reflexes were the reason why he didn't have a second and Newcastle looked very comfortable.

Then came Norwich. Second in the league, fearless, they hit back just before half-time through a penalty. Cameron Jerome – turning past Jonjo Shelvey – curled a second over the recalled Karl Darlow in front of the Gallowgate. Anxiety rising, St James' Park fell silent when Jacob Murphy's shot looped off the boot of Ciaran Clark and sailed past Darlow to make it 3-1.

At that point, Newcastle were 10th. Benitez turned to the dugout in exasperation. A double substitution: Mitrovic on for Mo Diame, Isaac Hayden for Jack Colback. Benitez, whose system of a single striker backed up by a number 10 was the bedrock of his plans that year, went for two up front. It was the system the supporters wanted; the formation he'd answered more questions about than any other. Head strong Benitez might be, but he'd noticed the space between Norwich's two centre-backs since half-time. His opposite number, Alex Neil, obviously sensed that his team's vulnerabilities could be masked by putting the pressure on Newcastle's back four. Now it was Benitez's turn to try it.

Newcastle had not come back from behind to win a game since December 13 the previous year, when they had improbably beaten Spurs at White Hart Lane. When asked to respond against Fulham, Wolves or Huddersfield they'd only mustered one goal. The questions about character were in the mail, ready to land at Benitez's doorstep at full-time.

Mitrovic had barely had time to introduce himself to Norwich's back four when Shelvey, from deep inside his own half, hit a 'hail Mary' pass with intent. Sebastien Bassong was tracking it but it dipped at the last, crucial moment. Gayle was on his shoulder. One touch, the ball under control and a right foot shot at pace past McGovern. It was so quick, you had to watch it again on slow motion to appreciate what Gayle had managed to pull of to score a goal as instinctive as any scored at St James' Park that season.

The mood changed in an instant. Nineteen minutes to chase Norwich, who proved obdurate enough to keep Newcastle at arm's length until the fourth official raised the board to signal seven minutes of injury time.

Five minutes into the seven, Gouffran – reviled and written off the previous season – headed a DeAndre Yedlin cross past McGovern. An untidy finish: a salvage complete.

Not quite. Sixty seconds later, another raking punt into the box. Mitrovic won his header, the ball landed at Gayle's quick feet. Two more touches and then a shot through a sea of legs. It was not the cleanest of hits but McGovern saw it late, dived to his right and watched it roll into the net.

Pandemonium at St James' Park. Gouffran pulled the ball from the net and hammered it high into the Tyneside sky. Mitrovic stalked a euphoric Gayle and wrestled him to the ground. Shelvey hauled nine-year-old ball boy Joshua Follin into the air. Up in the corporates, Norwich owner Delia Smith beat a hasty retreat. Canaries chairman Ed Balls, fresh from *Strictly Come Dancing* training, was more gracious. For Newcastle it felt like a critical, pivotal moment when belief returned. The Newcastle bench leapt to its feet but Benitez was not celebrating. He was as frantic as the rest of the stadium but still trying to get his message across to the players not to let Norwich find a way in the final 60 seconds.

At the end, the mask of composure slipped. Mitrovic, adrenaline still coursing through his veins, lifted Benitez off his feet in a bear hug. "How did he manage to pick me up?" Benitez laughed afterwards. He was not one for wild celebrations. Players usually kept a respectful distance. But this time he didn't mind. "He is a player who isn't playing but he has that reaction, which is good. We have to use his energy now in the right way," Benitez said.

When he needed to, Benitez had again found a solution. Newcastle's new team had found a way to answer those thudding questions about character and comebacks.

***

GAYLE scored 23 goals for Benitez over the course of the season – one every 93 minutes he was on the field. It might have been 30 if he'd not suffered a recurrence of the hamstring injury that had halted him in the previous campaign but, even with those caveats, he proved an inspired signing.

It was the furthest Gayle had gone north but he settled in instantly. Tynemouth beach, the fervour of St James' Park, the pressure – it was what he wanted.

Gayle worried at times during the season that he wasn't doing enough in games: was he involved enough in the build-up? Sky flashed up a statistic at one point in the campaign that showed other strikers who had scored fewer goals had double the number of touches over a game.

As long as the goals went in, it did not matter. Benitez supplied him with clips of other strikers, illustrating the way he imitated some of the best in the world. Gayle loved work. He gave his all in the gym and only seemed to break down when his schedule was disrupted by the birth of his daughter, Indie.

Again, Benitez handled the injuries delicately. The hamstring against Brentford in January was a concern but when he hobbled off against Aston Villa, it was more a case of mind over matter. Benitez did not order a scan: one of his bugbears with modern players was the need to find out through a scan what the problem was. For all athletes, tiny scars or tears are a fact of life. He was confident that the tests his medical team had already done showed Gayle could play on. The striker concurred. He came back and scored two crucial goals.

The Championship couldn't handle Gayle at full throttle. It was difficult, sometimes, to work out exactly what underpinned his brilliance in front of goal. Sky anchor Scott Minto, a full-back himself in his days before broadcasting, recognised something early in the season.

"It is his movement that is just unlike anything else. We pulled up a stat at Sky that said he had fewer touches than most of the strikers at Newcastle but his goalscoring rate was just fantastic.

"He doesn't need a lot of chances. That sounds obvious but what isn't is the way he moves. As a full-back you wouldn't like playing against a Gayle because you'd think you knew where he was and then, when a pass was played in, he'd have moved somewhere that then takes you off balance. How do you cope with that? Most of the Championship didn't seem to be able to."

It was September 28 when Gayle's intervention against Norwich arrived. Newcastle won every game until November 26. It was the first real sign of what was stirring underneath the Rafalution.

11. Trust And Intelligence

What Makes Rafa Benitez's Ideal Player

"It's the culture Rafa brings. Newcastle isn't a stepping stone anymore"

Isaac Hayden, May 2017

RAFA BENITEZ spent tens of millions, signed 12 players and fired the first shots in a revolution that transformed the squad and mentality at Newcastle. But one of the biggest players in those early days was also his smallest.

Vurnon Anita stands 5ft 6ins tall. A part-time, amateur rapper, he was among the most unassuming members of a squad that was undermined by its lack of loud voices before Benitez began to dismantle and rebuild the flawed culture that preceded him.

Anita was signed from Ajax in the summer that followed Newcastle's fifth-placed finish in 2012 and pitched straight into the battle of wills between chief scout Graham Carr and Alan Pardew. Carr recommended the midfielder for his versatility, technical ability and the fact that he could operate in several different positions. A £6.7m deal was struck but Pardew struggled to trust the player. He was dropped after January of his first season – Pardew wanted a more traditionally British central midfielder. When he asked for one, the request was blocked. He was told he already had a midfielder but Anita's craft and efficiency was sidelined.

In Benitez's world, Anita was prized for different reasons. When Newcastle's manager analysed the players he inherited, he recognised that there were things missing from the group. It needed bigger characters and more spirit. He wanted to reinforce the team with an English spine and Championship know-how. He was particularly strong on the latter point. But that did not mean that there was not room for an unsung hero like Anita if the deficit of chemistry could be addressed.

Benitez prizes intelligence in his players. Perhaps that is the result of his degree in physical education – he likes to teach and loves to see his players respond to his lessons.

A case in point: the moment he knew Newcastle would endure in the promotion race was when he had Isaac Hayden, the club's rising midfield star, knock on his office door at 9am on the day that followed their insipid defeat at Ipswich asking for advice on how to improve his personal contribution to the promotion effort. There was a fatigue about Newcastle's play at Portman Road as they lost 3-1 in East Anglia. Nerves contributed. The tension of playing under pressure was getting to an inexperienced group. But the thirst for knowledge remained.

Benitez was happy to run him through clip after clip about where it went wrong. Hayden – a strong character who sought Benitez's advice throughout the season – was the perfect emblem of the Spaniard's new model army.

The culture that Benitez wanted to have among his squad had to be honest, hard-working and prepared to learn. They were the qualities that accompanied the Spaniard into work every day. For all that he had achieved in the game – and his CV was a match for any coach in England plying their trade in the top flight, never mind the second tier – Benitez was not afraid to admit that he was learning from the experience of managing in a different way, in a different division. If that was the case for him, it was the minimum he expected of his players.

He certainly got that with the squad he put together at Newcastle. There was a thirst for knowledge that made Benton a football campus. "I want to improve and be the best I can," Hayden told *The Times* after the season concluded.

"Rafa's got the same drive and determination that I have. It's the culture that Rafa brings. He goes: 'Look, if you're not playing, it's because of you, not because of anyone else, not because of me, it's you. You've not done enough in training, or when you've performed, to make me want to keep you in the team.' He's fair. He'll give you a chance, a game, whether it's a cup game, 20 minutes, and you have to do something in that time to show him you want to play for Newcastle."

Before Benitez, there was a feeling that too many players stagnated at Newcastle. It was raised at boardroom level. Mike Ashley had asked, when the club was confronted with an injury crisis before a game at Norwich in 2011, why there weren't more players coming through the Academy to fill in.

There was no answer. It was an uncomfortable scenario for successive Newcastle managers.

Players had burst on to the scene and shone brightly at first. One was Gael Bigirimana, a Burundi-born midfielder tipped for England honours after Newcastle paid a six-figure sum to sign him from Coventry City. As a 19-year-old he played Premier League football for Newcastle but he was lost to the cause. Dropped from the first-team picture, he lost focus. Bigirimana had injury problems but he was not engaged. There was talent but as Pardew tried to fire-fight at Newcastle, he did not have time to worry about what was happening with the club's lost boys.

One of Benitez's skills was to engage everyone, even those who were not necessarily in his first-team thinking. He wanted players who had intelligence on and off-the-field. The preparatory work done in the summer that followed relegation had created a culture that imprinted professionalism, a hunger for knowledge and a desire to improve in its DNA.

Newcastle had some big names leading their promotion charge. But it was Anita's intelligence that intrigued and beguiled Benitez. "He's a professional," Benitez beamed when asked about the Netherlands international before the season began. "He is someone you can trust."

That was a key point. Benitez's preferred system was one that relied on discipline. There was room for improvisation to a point, but he needed players who would be able to carry out the orders that had been laid out for them in the days before the game.

Anita was one who Benitez took to immediately. The Netherlands man could play in either full-back slot, in the centre of midfield and also to the right of midfield. Before the first game of the season against Fulham, Benitez joked that if he was taller he would try him in goal.

"He's clever, he's someone that you can trust and I am very happy with him," Benitez said in those August days.

He played 31 times over the course of the season, much of it through pain. When the manager reflected on the story of the season after it finished, he made particular mention of the role that Anita had played.

In the cold, freezing and frayed days of January – when Newcastle needed to rediscover their winning form as the promotion race became constricting – Anita suffered a debilitating ankle injury during a narrow defeat of Brentford. He played through the pain. "He has showed his commitment," Benitez said.

***

BENITEZ'S Newcastle were a democracy – and not everyone would have appreciated what that meant. Talent was not always the most important currency for Benitez to trade in.

The case of Aleksandar Mitrovic consistently fascinated. He was the striker signed by Newcastle as a rough diamond – the club convinced by his tendency to emerge as a match-winner in big games. They had watched him playing for Anderlecht against Borussia Dortmund and Arsenal in the Champions League and noted his aggression, aerial ability and movement.

Background checks had revealed worrying signs of ill-discipline – his tendency to put on weight, his inability to control his emotions on the field – but there was a feeling that he could be controlled. Benitez looked like the perfect man to mould him into a striker of serious potential but a moment of madness – on the day when Newcastle unified behind the Spaniard – was to have serious ramifications for the Serbian.

Mitrovic had scored one and laid on another as Newcastle tore apart Tottenham on the final day of the 2015/16 Premier League season, but then lunged in on Kyle Walker. It was a straight red card offence – a foul that left no room for leniency. It meant that Newcastle had to play out the rest of the game with 10 men, while Mitrovic would face a three-game suspension for the first matches of the Championship season the following campaign.

Playing for other managers, Mitrovic might have found absolution early in the season. After all, the Serbian was seen by many opposition managers in the Championship as potentially Newcastle's greatest second-tier weapon.

But Benitez re-drew his entire plan for the early season based around a different set of strikers because of that. Mitrovic's inability to stay on the pitch in that final game of the season had cost him. That message – that small margins matter for strikers – was one that Mitrovic sometimes failed to heed, and was one of the main reasons why he struggled to find his way into the team.

There was a genuine warmth from the striker towards Benitez. "He is liked by the players – I have learned a lot from him," Mitrovic said of the manager. And he was one of the few who regularly breached the line between dressing room and dug-out.

After Newcastle beat Norwich, Mitrovic grabbed Benitez and hoisted him in the air. After promotion was achieved, it was Mitrovic who was the only person to spray Champagne over the manager. Benitez didn't mind. He was not the same man who had been accused of being distant by Steven Gerrard when the pair worked together at Anfield.

Benitez became frustrated by the continual talk that emanated from Mitrovic's agents about potential moves away. He knew that Mitrovic was happy and settled in Newcastle where his partner, Kristina, had given birth to his son, Luka. But there were people working around the forward who were prepared to move him on – both during the summer break and the January transfer window. In the latter, moves to Portugal and Italy were lined up for Mitrovic. Benitez flatly ruled them out.

Benitez would stick up for Mitrovic when he felt that the player was being judged by reputation. But the eagle-eyed observers noted that when Benitez picked a team to do a tactically disciplined job at Huddersfield in the March of that season, it was Daryl Murphy who he went for. Mitrovic ended the season with a smile but it was a learning curve.

He was not the only one to find out that talent alone was not enough to secure Benitez's favour. The £8m centre-back, Chancel Mbemba, was Newcastle's most talented defender. Strong, mobile and agile, Benitez asked the club's hierarchy to resist offers for a player who had emerged from the wreckage of the Premier League relegation with his reputation enhanced by his own personal performances.

But Mbemba was exiled from the team for long spells in the promotion campaign. Ciaran Clark, a player who executed Benitez's plans perfectly, usurped him in September and Mbemba had to wait until injuries during the run-in allowed him a chance to re-emerge.

The fact was that Mbemba was coasting at Newcastle. He had barely picked up the language in his first year: infected, perhaps, by the carelessness and ill-discipline that made the club's dressing room so difficult to control before Benitez arrived. The manager asked him to try to improve his linguistic skills. Communication was going to be key.

But it was tactical ill-discipline in Newcastle's 2-0 defeat to Wolves that sparked his fall from grace. Benitez sent the team out with instructions to play diagonal balls forward – the theory was to bypass the opposition midfield. He wanted Newcastle to go more direct.

Inside 20 minutes, Mbemba shipped possession four times. Benitez was infuriated that, on each occasion, it was because he had looked to pass the ball forward. On the half an hour, he put through his own net.

"The football decisions were wrong," Benitez said after that game. "We put ourselves under pressure." The message was not meant solely for Mbemba but there was frustration that underscored it. There was steel underneath Benitez's velvet revolution. Mbemba started only one game between then and April.

It said much that when he re-emerged there was a sharpness about Mbemba's game. His English had improved. His ability to carry out instructions had, too. Mbemba played in all five of Newcastle's run-in games – three of them ended in clean sheets.

***

THERE were stories of self-improvement all around at Newcastle. DeAndre Yedlin had one. He had agonised about dropping down from the Premier League, where he had a long-term contract with Tottenham, to the Championship with Newcastle. But the club had a "Premier League mentality".

Yedlin had struggled to cope with the sound and fury of English football at first. But, he told *Sports Illustrated* after the season ended, his mental strength came when he discovered Brian Tracy, a motivational speaker from Canada. Buoyed by the message of his book, *Maximum Achievement* – which he had found on Amazon – he began to note down his goals, one week out, two weeks out, a month out. He took responsibility for his own success. It created a "positive mindset" that helped Yedlin to flourish.

Benitez had created a culture that challenged and cajoled improvements out of his players. There were no favourites. Talent wasn't going to be enough.

12. All Together Now

Inside The Unseen Backroom Revolution

"It was not that everything was wrong before I got here"

Rafa Benitez, 2016

SIMON SMITH thought he was only popping in for a quick coffee with the manager.

It was early on in Rafa Benitez's time at Newcastle United. Smith had been appointed as the club's goalkeeper coach by Steve McClaren the previous summer, returning from an assignment to spot and coach the best young English goalkeeping talent. He had enjoyed working for the Football Association but come on, this was Newcastle United. His club.

There was a nervous energy at the training ground when Benitez arrived. Excitement, for the most part. But for the coaching staff who remained – Smith was one of only two survivors from

McClaren's backroom team – that feeling was mixed with trepidation. There would likely be new ideas, new theories. The worry was that might mean a new man.

His mind jumped back to the first time he'd been introduced to Sir Bobby Robson. Smith was first appointed by Sir Bobby's predecessor, Ruud Gullit, and did not know whether he was going to be kept on. First impressions matter. The meeting was a crucial one. He was greeted with a warm handshake and words that lived with him forever. "You don't know me and I don't know you but we'll give it a go and see how we get on," Sir Bobby told him. He laughed about it afterwards. The humility was disarming: there wasn't a single person in Tyneside who didn't know who Sir Bobby was. But the meeting had been quick, reassuring and with a nice subliminal message in there: stay on your toes, but get on with your job.

With Benitez, it couldn't have been more different. Their meeting went beyond the first coffee: Benitez engaging Smith on the finer technical aspects of the goalkeeper's craft. At one point, he was out of his chair, showing off stances that he feels give the best chance to make save.

Smith left impressed. "One of the things that I didn't expect when I met Rafa was his knowledge of goalkeeping. He has a real interest in it," he said.

Benitez's first job at Real Madrid was to coach the goalkeepers. He was a midfielder by trade so had studied how the first-team 'keepers did it. He had voraciously asked questions. He listened to the answers, formulated his own opinions. That file of notes locked away in his study somewhere was packed with information about how the very best honed their technique.

"He has a real knowledge and a great understanding of goalkeeping and the technique that goes into making a good 'keeper," Smith said.

"I didn't really expect that because, while I knew he had been a successful manager who had won things throughout his career, I didn't know he had that extra knowledge. Working with Sir Bobby was fantastic but his attitude was: 'You're my goalkeeping lad, you get on with it.' Rafa is different."

He asked Smith about the players he'd worked with. Shay Given was a brilliant goalkeeper: technically one of the most adept in the history of the Premier League. Ahead of his time. Steve Harper, another Newcastle great, unfortunate to play for the club at the same time as Given, was another topic of conversation.

Smith, a genial, likeable coach, walked away impressed.

***

WHEN Benitez won the Championship Manager of the Month award for October, one of the more obvious decisions that the English Football League made during a season of contentious calls, he had a problem.

The award arrived after a month in which Newcastle had won six in a row. Rotherham were dispatched to start the month, Newcastle navigating their way past the worst team in the division on a day when they performed above themselves. Brentford – a club owned by professional gambler Matthew Benham, who have attempted to use cutting edge scientific techniques to level the Championship's budgetary inequities – were next up, beaten 3-1 at St James' Park.

Gayle scored twice in successive matches, helping Newcastle to beat Barnsley 2-0 in front a packed, delighted away end at Oakwell. The entire squad – substitutes and all – made straight for the supporters after every goal that night. After the disappointments of recent seasons, it felt like the moment the players and the travelling army who followed them cemented their burgeoning relationship. It was a big moment on-the-pitch: the first time Newcastle topped the league.

Ipswich and Preston – first in the League Cup and then in a much tougher Championship away game – were beaten with 11 goals scored to their opponents' one. Newcastle were top and looked like they belonged there.

But Benitez wanted the pictures that went out with the award to reflect the collective effort that had gone into them. He wanted his backroom team to be in the shot, touching the award to show it was for all of them. Smith, though, had been laid low with a virus. Benitez did not want him to be left out. It was all or nothing. If you screw your eyes and look closely enough at the picture that went out with the press release, you can see the solution. Smith is in the picture, photoshopped into the background with a broad smile on his face. He got some stick for that.

That is how Benitez does things. All together. It is why the people who work with him and have followed him from Liverpool to Chelsea, Milan to Napoli and Madrid are so important. They are a window into his management technique and have been crucial in helping to rebuild Newcastle.

For Benitez, it was not just the coaches he brought in who were important. At Newcastle he is the conductor, arranging regular meetings with the Academy and medical staff. He wants to know about the media strategy and was consulted on designs for the home kit towards the end of the promotion season. When he was a younger manager that interest would have extended to every facet of the club he was in charge of. He would have wanted to be the one making all of those decisions.

He arrived at Newcastle a different man and a different manager from the one who had worked under Vincent del Bosque as Real's assistant boss. Now he increasingly recognised the importance of empowering those underneath him and that meant that the staff he inherited – from the medical department to the goalkeeping coach, the kit man and the press officers – had to be on board.

As much as there was excitement at Newcastle at what was to

come, there is always a sense of foreboding at regime change. Relegation meant all of those things were compounded. When a team drops down a division it means revenues are cut, budgets have to be revised. It is rarely the playing staff who are left out of pocket when the results go south: more often than not it is those on modest salaries who have mortgages to pay who are forced to leave the club.

At Newcastle, that was exactly what happened when the team were relegated in 2010. When Benitez negotiated to stay at Newcastle – after days of talks – one of the things the club had resolved to do was invest rather than cut. No-one who didn't want to leave would have to in that summer. Instead, the club brought people in: a former local newspaper editor, Brian Aitken, was given a role as head of corporate affairs, asked to dip into his contacts book to help bridge the gap between the business community and the club. It was a shrewd move by the club.

"We recognise that we need to do more," Charnley said in that announcement. Aitken rightly pin-pointed the feel-good factor of the Benitez appointment as a key to putting Newcastle at the heart of the vibrant entrepreneurial culture of the North East.

It was a world away from the antagonism of the recent past. Newcastle had not been afraid of picking fights previously: not least after the stadium was renamed the Sports Direct Arena in a move that prompted enough outcry for the city's council to write to the media urging them not to use the name. Then chief executive Derek Llambias' letter to the council leader accused them of a 'cheap publicity stunt' and threatened legal action if money was lost as a result of it. These were draining, damaging battles.

In the Benitez era, engagement was the key. He was not directly responsible for these changes to the corporate structure of the club but they were ushered in on a wave of momentum that he had inspired. The way that he had embraced the club and its history meant that these doors were being opened again. People wanted to talk to them again: everyone wanted to be associated with Benitez's Newcastle. They were looking upward and outward once more. Every person who worked for the club recognised that.

When the three points had been secured against Preston to clinch promotion in the penultimate home game of the season, there was a moment that typified Benitez's approach after the final whistle. He moved from player to player, taking time to shake all of their hands in gratitude at what they had achieved. But he also sought out the kit man, the club doctor, the ground staff, the club photographer, the pitch-side security. Over the course of the season, he had emphasised the need for everyone to come into work and do everything they could for the cause. He had guaranteed that if they did that, he would do the same. In a moment of glory and validation for him, there was time to recognise the contribution of everyone else.

"When I arrived it was not like everything was bad," he said, halfway through the season.

"I don't want to be unfair to anyone. We're all part of it: the analysis department, the communications department, the groundstaff – we have a lot of people here doing a great job. Everyone here is giving everything."

He recognised that there had to be a human touch to the way the club engaged with its people. Bridging the gap between community and club made sense. It meant that he could get to work in the way he wanted. And so could those close to him.

***

BENITEZ recognised that Newcastle's fans saw him as the figurehead of something different that was unfolding at their football club. He knew that he was anointed as an "idol" after relegation. It was a pressure, but one that he shared with some old friends.

The backroom team that Benitez assembled at Newcastle was

close-knit. His two first-team coaches for the Championship season, Antonio Gomez Perez and Mikel Antia, both played for Benitez at the Real Madrid Academy.

Perez's story was fairly typical. Benitez might have been portrayed as aloof or confrontational in England because he stood up to what he saw as the cadre of managers who were allies of Sir Alex Ferguson, but that was not the experience of those who have known him in Spain.

When Perez played under Benitez at Madrid, he remembers being so inspired by the sessions put on by the young Academy coach that he rushed home to write them down in a folder that he still refers to today. Benitez was successful, too. His Real Madrid under-19 side beat Barcelona to win the Copa del Rey in his first year. It was an eye-catching triumph: his young charges were fascinated by Benitez's obsession with shape, strategy and the way he probed opponents' weaknesses.

"Rafa thinks about football 24/7," Gomez says. "But he is very generous. He is very loyal. He expects you to work hard but, in return for that, you can ask him anything."

When Perez retired from playing he went to work for Albacete's youth team. Benitez, by then, was one of La Liga's hottest coaching talents, attempting to break the dominance of Spain's biggest two clubs with Valencia. The pair met after the two teams played each other, talking tactics and football in the manager's room.

"I will always remember that. There aren't many people in football prepared to give away their secrets like that," Perez said. He was delighted when Benitez asked him to join his Liverpool coaching staff. He is now Newcastle's head of analysis.

Over the course of the 2016/17 season, Benitez repeated those conversations with other young and experienced managers across the Championship.

Antia had also played for Benitez and replaced the Italian Fabio Pecchia, a smart coach with a legal degree who had brought intensity to his coaching staff at Napoli and then Real Madrid. Pecchia joined Hellas Verona in Italy's Serie B before the Championship season began – a blow to Benitez but one that he understood came with the territory.

"When a coach of yours wants to move on to become a manager, you have to let them. It is an exciting opportunity. You cannot stand in their way," he says. Ian Cathro, the serious, deadpan Scot who he had inherited from McClaren, followed Pecchia into front-line management – taking a job at Hearts in the middle of the season.

Antia had joined from the Aspire Academy in Doha, where they are building towards the 2022 World Cup, hoping to bring through a generation of Qatari footballers who can compete at international level. At Newcastle the demand was instant. When he was appointed, Benitez gave him a brief to look after set pieces – having watched hundreds of hours of footage of the Championship and recognised that this was an area where Newcastle would have to be razor-sharp.

It worked. Newcastle had been one of the poorest teams in the country from dead balls in the years before Benitez arrived, scoring just eight in the season they went down. It became a running joke when they went from the autumn of 2011 to 2013 without scoring from a corner. It ran to 494 corners before Loic Remy ended one of the longest runs in professional football, much to the relief of Alan Pardew.

In the Championship season, Newcastle scored from set pieces 21 times. They were well-drilled, both to attack and defend them. From direct free-kicks they scored four times: on each occasion it was a different player who converted. No team in the division scored as many the way that Newcastle did. It was another small piece of the jigsaw.

His assistant manager and fitness coach was the man he knew as 'Paco' – Francisco de Miguel Moreno. He is the only one of the coaching staff that Benitez brought to Newcastle who has not played professionally but Benitez's prizes his background in physical fitness and medicine. He has a degree in PE and an infectious enthusiasm for the job. Moreno had considered joining the army and then the navy, but loved sport too much. He worked for the INEF in Madrid, the faculty of sciences for physical activity and sport before joining a small club in Spain. He took a variety of jobs prior to moving to Valencia, where he met Benitez.

In England, fitness coaches drill the players. They work on strength and conditioning before a manager steps in to take tactical work. With Moreno it was different – "Something in between, not like your typical fitness coach in England," he said – and it seemed to work for Newcastle.

It worked like this: Moreno was Benitez's 'big picture' man. He had to be obsessive about data, collecting the opinions of the coaches on how the players had performed in training sessions, and mixing it with analysis of the sessions that came from GPS devices and heart rate monitors worn by the players.

All of this information was fed into an index that was updated every day. Every fortnight or so Benitez would review it and decide whether changes needed to be made to the sessions.

Moreno linked in with the medical department and also the club's analysts, planning training sessions for Benitez partly based on who the club's next opponents were. And when the need arose, he also took coaching sessions.

He said: "You cannot train people for fitness without the logic of the game. You always have to train, considering the logic of the game which includes thinking tactically, technically, physically – you have to put them all together. It's good to have the full control of 'the load'.

"You have the big picture of everything. Sometimes in England, the fitness coach has a difficult job. Maybe they have 20 minutes before a session or two days a week when they have a window to work. It's not the best scenario, in my opinion. It's much better when you can work together with the rest and say: 'OK, we have to create something together'."

He was full of ideas. Based on years of working with elite players, he'd felt they were more at risk of injury when they were at peak fitness. He preferred it when they were at 85 per cent fitness, which dictated why some players were pulled away from harder duties in sessions, or rested altogether.

All of the stats, the analysis, the data and the hunches based on the trained eye were compressed into a 45-minute team talk that Benitez would deliver to the team the day before games. Short, sharp, concise – he did not want to overload the players.

With 46 league games and a few more in the cups it was a sizeable workload. But Benitez wanted to approach Burton Albion the same way he did Barcelona. No corners were to be cut.

It required the coaches working all together. It helped that they liked each other, pulling long days with Benitez and ordering in food. The football broke up sometimes to play 'Mus' but this was not a Spanish team imposing their culture on the club.

Sure, there were a few new ideas – Smith was advised to record his goalkeeper training sessions and use the video suite to analyse them – but they also wanted to integrate. Pinned up on the wall, there was a list of Geordie phrases that they all had to learn. 'Paco' went to the Northumberland countryside to ride his mountain bike.

They all worked in the same office. Voices were never raised. "The Newcastle experience is something new for us," said Gomez. "It is fantastic to work with the supporters 100 per cent behind you, as part of a great city and a club that wants success.

"People may ask, 'Why Newcastle?' after what we had done before. But Rafa is happy here."

***

WHEN Benitez arrived at Newcastle, one of the first things he noted was the club's lengthy injury list. With Newcastle facing a season in the Championship, that had to change.

For Dr Paul Catterson, the change in culture was marked. A Liverpool season-ticket holder before he moved to Newcastle to train in medicine, Catterson's background was in Accident & Emergency, dealing with car crashes or serious incidents. It was quite the change in pace when he took up an invitation to come and work Newcastle's reserve team at weekends.

He had worked under previous managers: promoted while Alan Shearer was the manager before experiencing the work of Chris Hughton, Pardew, John Carver and Steve McClaren, too.

Benitez was different. He took a serious interest in medicine and one of his first calls every morning was to Catterson to talk about the players and their condition. Communication improved between the coaching and medical departments: Benitez arranged for two Spanish physios to join the department and bring in a Continental philosophy to rehabilitation.

Catterson said that there was an increased "harmony" between the departments. No players were rushed back quicker than they needed to be. Newcastle had injuries but they lost fewer days to problems than they had in the past.

"I strongly believe that the main thing is the culture that comes from the manager. The way he communicates with everybody is brilliant – from the kitchen staff to his most senior staff," Catterson said. "He looks all of us in the eye in the morning and you really get that connection. So, for me, everything that is going well off-the-field is being replicated on it."

Benitez healed those old wounds. He even found room for a cup run, making sure Newcastle addressed one of the supporters' biggest bugbears. After two more league wins – over Cardiff City and then a thoroughly professional dispatching of Leeds United at Elland Road – Newcastle lost to Blackburn, and then faced

Premier League Hull City in the EFL Cup quarter-final. A semi-final was beckoning when Newcastle led in extra-time, but Robert Snodgrass equalised Mo Diame's 98th-minute opening goal almost immediately.

Penalties went against Newcastle: frustration but an element of pride. Unlike in previous years, the deflation was not because Newcastle had not tried. Benitez promised the club would be back. The fans believed.

13. Referees And Setbacks

Confronting The Mid-Season Problems

"We try to respect the referees but still I don't know what is going on"

Rafa Benitez, 2017

RAFA BENITEZ would look out on the crowd of journalists at Real Madrid and anticipate the landmines being placed before him with every fresh question.

Sometimes, the queries seemed innocuous enough. At other times, he knew the questions arrived with a venom that might have been planted by someone other than the journalists who delivered them. To Benitez, this must have felt like another one of those games of chess from his boyhood days – the art of saying just enough to inform without manoeuvring himself into a position from which his enemies could overwhelm him. Even for someone who loved finding solutions, this must have seemed the most desperate type of fire fighting. Real Madrid is some club but, beneath the facade, it can sometimes seem like a nest of vipers.

The football press conference can often seem like the most benign of assignments for the modern manager. At its worst, it becomes an exercise in banality. But when a club is as riven by factions as the modern-day Real, the challenge is to box clever. It did not take Benitez long to realise this was just another battle in the war to win over his Bernabeu doubters.

At one of the biggest clubs in the world, everyone seems to have an interest. In the far corner, one journalist might be aligned with the President. Another might have the ear of an out-of-favour player. Perhaps the medical staff had allied themselves with another. Benitez knew the agenda was rarely simple.

If the press pack was tough, the dressing room was almost impossible. Benitez had been offered the job as the most qualified man available, someone whose tactical acumen could give Real the edge in their tussles with Barcelona and city neighbours Atletico.

Perhaps, on paper, there was some logic to the appointment. Benitez's long history with Real meant that he understood the rivalries that defined the club – its need to not only win games, but to also aspire to a standard that had been set by the men who came before. Surely it followed that he would know the demands of the supporters because he had been one of them? But a cursory glance at Benitez's management modus operandi, and the way Real must be managed might have given a few hints at the problems that arrived almost as soon as his appointment was announced.

Benitez saw Barcelona and envied not their tika-taka football or the way they had beguiled the world with their style, but their consistency. Of course, Barca's football felt like artistry on its good days but it was also – crucially – winning football. In the seven years that preceded Benitez's appointment, Barcelona had won five titles and Real just one. They had the trophies to back up their beauty. Real were hardly serial losers but it felt like there was room for humility. It explains why he took an assignment that proved an impossible mission.

From the start, he was on the back foot. A manager prepared to duck and weave with the best of them appointed to one of the most political football clubs in the world? It never felt a good fit. For Benitez to do the job the way he wanted, Real's superstars would have to check their egos in at the door. Given all they had achieved before he arrived, it was never a realistic prospect.

The supporters did not recognise Benitez as one of their own. The media questioned his appointment almost as soon as it was announced. He was jeered in pre-season as he tested systems and formations in a game against Turkish club, Galatasaray.

To survive, Benitez would have to compromise. Results, if they arrived, would provide the insurance against the politics.

Real was, after all, the club Benitez could not say no to. He had wanted to return to England to be closer to his family – indeed, he had been a few hours away from signing the contract drawn up by David Gold and Karen Brady to take over at West Ham – but this club was part of his DNA. The first of his 1,000 games in management came in charge of Real Madrid's youth side.

Perhaps the war could not be won. If the smoothest of operators, Carlo Ancelotti, another of his generation's managerial greats, was not able to survive long despite a Champions League win and carrying the dressing room with him, what chance did Benitez have of creating a legacy? That was not the gig in Spain's capital. No manager had been able to build a dynasty like the one Pep Guardiola constructed at the Nou Camp, and Benitez was realistic enough to know that was not what was on offer. Still, he felt he deserved better than what was to come.

The players bristled against Benitez's training methods – and rebelled when he tried to break up cliques he felt were undermining the club. Journalists questioned his decisions. Supporters, eventually, gave him the indignity of the white handkerchief treatment.

His name was booed before his final game against Real Sociedad, a match that came a few short weeks after a 4-0 defeat in an El Clasico in which the attacking line-up he fielded bore little resemblance to the management philosophy honed in those years hunched over a notebook, squeezing every last detail from his training sessions at Extremadura, Valencia and Tenerife. The team picked that day was the one the President told him to play.

Despite the politics and the preening, he left with a 68 per cent win ratio. They were unbeaten as they moved into the knock-out phase of the Champions League. Stripped of context, it might sound impressive, but the year damaged Benitez. They were not good days. His reputation in Spain took a big dent.

Later, during a punditry gig with BT during his brief hiatus, he had the chance to reflect. "I was very proud to have the job, coming from Real Madrid's Academy.It was a shame what happened. It's a pity that we are not at the club anymore.

"To understand why it happened, you have to look at what has happened over the last years at Real. Camacho, Del Bosque, Mourinho, Ancelotti – it's not easy to be the manager there. You have to do everything perfectly. As soon as you do anything wrong or the chairman thinks it is wrong, you will have a problem.

"My assistant, Fabio Pecchia, said that you have the 'permanent presence' of the chairman. He is around. He is talking with the players, he's talking with the media so he's always around and it's not easy for a manager. It's not easy when you come from an experience like England, to see the chairman talking with the players or the press every single day."

At Newcastle, Benitez had escaped from the political machinations that saw him compromise his beliefs. But the North East did not bring serenity. Even in the Championship, at a club where he had won hearts as well as minds, a new set of problems had to be confronted, eventually. Politics were not confined to the marbled halls of the Bernabeu.

Newcastle had previous. The Mike Ashley era had thrown up some bizarre sights. Newcastle was a club riven by factions. Former boss Alan Pardew and chief scout Graham Carr were engaged in a barely concealed cold war for much of their time together. Pardew would not play Vurnon Anita because he did not think him good enough. Carr stood firm that he was good enough, and Newcastle would not sign a replacement. It was not healthy.

Pardew had made the ultimate power play after Joe Kinnear was appointed as director of football, seeking to use the situation to consolidate his own influence. He called North East journalists to an under-the-radar lunch by Newcastle's Quayside and over pizza, sparkling water and Peroni, he spelled out his intentions. He made it very clear he wanted to bring in more British players – he wanted to sign striker Darren Bent and Sunderland's right-back, Phil Bardsley. Neither player arrived.

In January, Benitez had to confront issues of his own at Newcastle – internal and external. He knew that if he allowed these issues to overwhelm him, his reputation in England would be tarnished. The bitter Bernabeu experience informed his reaction to the problems stalking the Championship's sleeping giant.

***

COMPARED to life at Real, Benitez found himself largely out of the glare of the national and international spotlight at Newcastle.

It was not that he had lost his star power or that he was enjoying some sort of Championship career gap year. Far from it: in Newcastle, he found the hopes of the city's supporters projected on to him and that carried a burden that Benitez took seriously. But from a national perspective, the Championship plays second fiddle to the Premier League and the coverage reflects that.

Some big, historic clubs are beached in the Championship and Newcastle's Spanish stardust in the dug-out did not make them an exception to that fact. Relegation meant that press conferences at Newcastle were far from the political minefield that he had encountered in Spain.

Benitez communicated his message well. He had understood the importance of using media appearances to offer a pretty consistent message. But when he needed to make a point, he was not afraid to create headlines – almost as much by what he left out as by what he actually said. It was a smart balancing act. Some seasoned Benitez watchers might call it politics, as usual. In a memorable column that spoke fondly of the way Benitez worked, Jamie Carragher called the Spaniard the most political manager he'd ever met. Benitez laughed it off, saying he preferred to work without complications. But that was different from not knowing how to play a situation to his advantage if it came up.

Football's media landscape has changed beyond all recognition in the decade since Benitez first moved to England to take over at Liverpool. Even as recently as 10 years ago, the written press would have dictated the agenda, deciding on the questions and lines to take before any given game. Broadcast media's influence had grown with Sky's investment in the sport and the channel's rolling sports news station – an unexpected, runaway success – had hours to fill, poring over the minutiae of the game. But even back in 2007, few would have predicted the growth in social media that would shift the dynamic of the way the sport was presented.

By 2017, the social media sites Twitter and Instagram had, perhaps, a disproportionately sizeable influence over the agenda. A rogue or deliberately placed post could shape the news cycle for days at a time and the savvier of the players understood that. In Madrid, many of the stars that Benitez had dropped or had judged in no condition to play would take to posting pictures of themselves training hard in the gym for their followers. The effect was to subtly undermine the authority of the manager.

In England, football had seemed slow to adapt to social media at first – perhaps not appreciating the transformative impact it was having on the sport. But at Newcastle, thanks to Joey Barton's early adoption of the medium to shift perceptions of him, they knew only too well that it carried resonance. Barton's furious tweet storm at Elland Road in 2011 led to him being released by Newcastle – at a cost to a club that had grown tired of his rebellious streak playing out over cyberspace.

The mainstream media had also changed since Benitez's time at Liverpool. With traditional circulation figures dropping, local and national titles increasingly recognised the importance of the digital market. It sparked a huge growth in sports journalism – but not necessarily in the way that managers had anticipated.

A whole industry was reshaping under the nose of football's old guard and perhaps they didn't realise that the audience was changing: becoming smarter in some ways, but also more immediate. Alan Pardew spoke of the way social media was changing the demands of the football manager, and he had a point. The focus was shifting: management was now no longer just about affecting what goes on during 90 minutes on a Saturday, but also being across issues that are a product of a furious and unrelenting news cycle. At Newcastle, Lee Charnley has a Twitter account but not in his own name. Benitez, by contrast, had a Twitter account and website that was run on his behalf. "Use it to communicate, not to interact," he counselled his players after Matz Sels deleted his Twitter account following abuse.

At Real Madrid, he'd seen players using social media to portray a certain image of themselves when that wasn't always the case. He hated the window social media gave on the dressing room. "You don't like the people to know in your job; your job, my job, any job, but it's already in the media, then fans know and they give their opinion and everything changes now, whereas before it was more closed off," he said.

The Spaniard was not a regular social media surfer although

his two daughters kept him updated on what was being said. Although traditionalists would argue that this was denigrating the game, there was a democratisation at play here. The paying public had previously been solely consumers but now they had the power to shape the sporting agenda through social media.

Some things never changed: the local media in Liverpool and Newcastle retain a sizeable influence. When Benitez's future was up for debate at the end of the season, the *Chronicle's* campaign to keep him included an online petition and an open letter on the front page of the newspaper. Privately, Benitez acknowledged that this had helped sway his decision – and it was a stark contrast to the ban on local 'papers that made life difficult for Pardew. Benitez was a big enough name to make national headlines but he recognised the importance of the *Echo* in Liverpool and *The Chronicle* in Newcastle. He reads a lot of what is being written.

The Championship meant there was less national attention, especially during the autumn time when Newcastle's winning run removed some of the shock factor that had been so compelling in the early weeks of the season. A typical press conference for Benitez at Newcastle in the Premier League would have seen the North East football writers for every national title attend. In the Championship those numbers dropped, not least because David Moyes – newly installed at Sunderland – tended to hold his media day at roughly the same time.

The cameras of Sky Sports – football's paymasters – are the prime players and take precedent. They get first jab at questions before the local broadcasters ask the questions. The answers to those are not embargoed – which usually means a flurry of tweets straight after Benitez's press conference.

Local radio stations get a separate briefing, as does *The Chronicle* and then the traditional morning titles – Newcastle's *Journal* as well as the national newspapers – are the final port of call. Benitez recognised the power of the medium and was comfortable with it. He was a busy man but off-the-record anecdotes, about past adventures with Liverpool or other clubs, often extended the briefings further into the afternoon. It felt a long way from the lock out that greeted Steve McClaren's introduction, and the preferred media partner initiative that had brought that controversy to the fore was quietly dropped in Benitez's first full season. Credit where it was due, the club seemed to be learning lessons.

Benitez remained restless. The Championship's fixture list was unrelenting and there were several signposts for the unease that was to follow, not least when a controversy bubbling beneath the surface became public in November.

After a testy home defeat against Wolves in September, visiting players alleged Jonjo Shelvey had used racially-charged language towards Romain Saiss as tempers frayed during the 2-0 defeat. It had been an early taster of how Newcastle would be viewed in the division: there was a feeling in United's camp that the celebrations of Wolves' manager, Walter Zenga, had been a touch too provocative. Shelvey – a firebrand character with a short trigger – had been in a running battle with Wolves players throughout the game but the allegations that followed were very serious. Benitez was informed immediately by the referee, Tim Robinson, but Shelvey contested that he had used Saiss' ethnicity to insult him.

The matter went to an FA panel, who levied a charge on Newcastle's best player in November. A hearing was scheduled for December but the punishment hanging over Shelvey was a five-game ban. Considering his importance to Newcastle's cause, it was a potential headache for the club at a time when their progress seemed unerring.

Still, there was little to suggest the City Ground storm that was waiting for Newcastle in the first week of December – a potentially pivotal month for any Championship promotion pretenders. Newcastle's defeat to Blackburn Rovers had been put down to changes the manager had made for the midweek match at Hull

City in the EFL Cup quarter-final. Newcastle had narrowly lost that game on penalties but, on a Friday night in the East Midlands, they had the opportunity to stretch their lead at the top of the second tier.

***

BENITEZ had been nursing a heavy cold in the days before the Nottingham Forest match, his voice straining in the training sessions that preceded the evening engagement. Little that happened that night helped.

The City Ground might not shine like some of the newer Championship grounds but, what it lacks in modern facilities it more than makes up for in soul. Wooden chairs still clatter in the Main Stand: *Mull of Kintyre* is sung lustily before kick-off. When Newcastle came to town, the atmosphere had an edge.

United began well, dictating the play. Shelvey did not seem cowed by the added attention: he was central to everything that the visitors did so well as they dominated possession and tempo. Benitez's team pressed. Matt Ritchie went close. It seemed only a matter of time before they broke the deadlock.

The first flash-point changed the game. Henri Lansbury, a player whose rich potential was nurtured at Arsenal's Academy, was leading the home side's resistance and was the main source of danger for Newcastle's defence. His running battle with Shelvey was a fascinating sub-plot but, when the two tussled just after the half-hour mark, referee Steve Martin produced a red card for Newcastle's outstanding player.

It seemed harsh. Shelvey was pulled to the ground by Lansbury and, wriggling to get away from his protagonist, there was a brief connection with his boot. Lansbury's reaction seemed incendiary but the referee saw enough to send the United midfielder off. The offence was also in the penalty area but the prospect of a double blow was averted when Karl Darlow – against his former club – saved the resultant penalty, magnificently, diving to his left to deny Nicklas Bendtner.

Newcastle rallied. Ciaran Clark saw a goal disallowed for a marginal call on a foul in the penalty area but the pressure was building. Ritchie handed the tireless visitors the lead with a wonderful dipping shot in the last minute of the first half. The character imbued in Newcastle by their manager appeared to be shining through in adversity.

A second penalty and red card changed that in first-half stoppage-time. Lansbury again found wriggle room, drifting behind Paul Dummett to latch on to a through ball. The tangle of feet saw Lansbury collapse to the ground and Dummett dismissed for preventing a goalscoring opportunity. Unbelievably, Darlow saved from 12 yards again, preventing Lansbury from levelling matters by diving to his right before claiming Ben Osborn's header from the rebound.

Nine against 11, Newcastle showed impressive resolve. But their rearguard action was not enough. Bendtner's equaliser early in the second half prompted the hosts to launch a wave of attacks that Newcastle repelled until the 86th minute. Jamaal Lascelles' own goal, another player returning to the City Ground, was the final twist of the knife.

Newcastle's unease about refereeing in the Championship preceded that night. It boiled over as Benitez broke a promise not to single out officials publicly. "All the decisions went against us," he said. "The referees need to have more experience."

He accused Lansbury of "acting", calling for The FA to make an example of him. On the pitch, the Forest player said Shelvey had "lashed out". The match had turned on the decisions of Martin, an official who had spent most of his refereeing career bouncing between the second and third tier of English football.

In the dressing room, there was anger. Shelvey and Dummett

raged at the injustice. Newcastle's third defeat in six days was by far the hardest to take for players who already nursed a sense of grievance about the way they were being treated by officials.

Over the course of the season, there was dialogue with the authorities about the standards that Newcastle encountered. Benitez wondered why some Newcastle challenges were punished while similar tackles by teams they played were not penalised. In his research on the division he had been warned about the physicality of the league and the inconsistency of officials in the second tier – and perhaps that played on his mind as Newcastle encountered some bizarre, high-profile mistakes.

Martin's error-strewn evening in the East Midlands was just one case that he took to the authorities. He felt Newcastle had been on the wrong end of too many penalty decisions. Privately, he pointed to an earlier game in the season when Newcastle – outplaying Ipswich – had Dwight Gayle upended by goalkeeper Bartosz Bialkowski. He was later to respond in astonishment when referee Keith Stroud misinterpreted the rules and awarded a free-kick to Burton Albion after encroachment on a Ritchie penalty.

It may have sounded like the ventings of a conspiracy theorist to rivals in the Championship but Newcastle's appeals on the decisions which resulted in both Nottingham Forest penalty-kicks were successful. Dummett and Shelvey had their red cards rescinded and Martin was kept away from Newcastle games for the rest of the season. Similarly, Stroud faced a two-month suspension after his mistake made international headlines.

Viewed through that prism, Newcastle's manager formulated his own response to the way the season was starting to progress. Increasingly, his perception was that Newcastle were having to exert more effort than other teams because the entire division was stalking them. Benitez would point out the number of times rival managers would speak afterwards about their team playing their finest match of the season against his side. He told his team not to expect any favours – to make sure they were in control of their own destiny, not to leave anything to the officials or to chance.

He had other allies. Learned voices said that Newcastle games were becoming increasingly difficult to referee: that the pressure was being compounded by mistakes that their colleagues made. The former head of the Professional Game Match Officials Limited Group, Keith Hackett, voiced his concerns about the standard of officiating in the Championship. He called for Premier League referees to be re-assigned to cover Newcastle games to allay fears about officials' competence.

Part of Benitez's complaints were about consistency. He knew the rules inside out and wanted to know why they weren't being applied in the way he was used to.

Benitez was frustrated; down but not out. He saw a chance to rally supporters who had perhaps become a shade complacent at the way wins had been racked up so regularly. Discreet feelers were put out to communicate the message that Newcastle's supporters needed to know that they were everyone's prize target in the Championship. His response was to try and whip up a siege mentality at St James' Park.

The immediate response was peerless: three wins. Newcastle thrashed Birmingham 4-0 in front of a fired-up crowd of 52,145. Gayle's hat-trick swiped the headlines but Shelvey was the architect – his performance in the heart of midfield hinting at a player starting to assert his class in the Championship. Benitez was doubly pleased. He felt that intensity and unity could carry Newcastle towards 100 points if outside factors did not check their progress.

Two away victories – against the division's bantamweights Wigan and Burton, the latter victory especially hard-fought – teed the club up for Christmas. But a hearing at a solicitor's office in Birmingham was to have a lasting impact.

Shelvey's hearing shone a light on the less savoury side of the sport. In front of a three-man panel made up of former professionals Tony Agana and Gareth Farrelly – now a trainee solicitor himself – and David Casement QC, the events of a difficult afternoon at St James' Park were played out again.

Shelvey was one of several players who gave evidence. Wolves' Dominic Iorfa, Cameron Borthwick-Jackson and Matt Doherty all said they'd heard Newcastle's man use Saiss' ethnic origin in an abusive manner. Shelvey's lawyer argued that they'd misheard.

It was a lengthy hearing. Both sides disputed the account of the other. At one point the panel heard that Shelvey had called Iorfa a "peasant", and had made reference to his earnings. The hearing's written reasons noted this was a process known as "cashing him off" – a new term for most of the paying public.

Contentious though it might have been, the panel found The FA's case was proven. A five-match suspension was levied on Shelvey. It cost him £100,000 and he would also have to attend an education course. Shelvey toyed with an appeal. He maintained that he did not say it. "I am very disappointed and frustrated," he said in a statement. Benitez did not punish his midfielder but they decided not to appeal it. It was a big moment.

In the second city, without a ball being kicked, the next phase of Benitez's Rafalution was forced into action. If the first part had been serene and successful, the second was to become more fraught, tense and testing. Shelvey's suspension forced Newcastle's manager to become more pragmatic. It was arguably a greater triumph to emerge from that period unscathed than it was to sail the momentum of the spring in Championship ascendancy.

Benitez had left nothing to chance in this Championship season. But this was an unexpected and potentially damaging blow. With Mo Diame, Christian Atsu and Chancel Mbemba due to depart for the Africa Cup of Nations in January, Shelvey's extended absence created a void in midfield that was unwelcome with the games to come. The upcoming transfer window became all the more important.

14. January Blues

How Rafa Benitez Dealt With The Club's Internal Politics

"From this day forward, we will be making our own luck"

Mike Ashley, 2015

ON a May afternoon in 2015, the heat from a warm sun bathed the pitch at St James' Park. Blue skies stretched over Tyneside but a dark cloud hung over the club. Just over a year before Rafa Benitez entered the managerial fray, Newcastle United had arrived at another crossroads.

The club had been ambling along safely in the upper reaches of mid-table when Lee Charnley, having looked for a suitable replacement, decided to hand John Carver the job of succeeding Alan Pardew. Carver, a boyhood Newcastle fan with good coaching credentials, was regarded as a safe pair of hands by Charnley. But, by the end of a fraught season, they were dicing with danger. A collapse in form that neither Carver, nor a sub-standard playing staff were able to arrest had brought them to a decisive final day: victory over West Ham – managed by Sam Allardyce, who else – would guarantee Premier League football. Defeat would leave the door open for Hull City. Adrenaline surged through the city.

Inside the ground in the hours before kick-off, intrigue was piqued by what had happened in London a few days before the game. Mike Ashley had been holding court with a few friends over drinks. The desperate situation at Newcastle, his club, was chewed over.

It sounds odd to recount it now. If an asset that you own seems to be failing, why not step in and put it right? But that is to misunderstand the dynamic of Ashley's ownership of Newcastle. This is his club, but his front-line involvement in its running is fleeting and occasional. It is also perplexing.

As far back as 2013, Ashley was telling friends that what he hoped was that Newcastle would take care of itself without the need for him to be 'hands-on' in his approach. The theory seemed to be that by putting people in charge of the club who knew his overall aim for it, and who were competent enough to run it properly, they would generate enough money for him not to have put any money into the club, as he had when he bought it or saw it relegated in 2009.

Ashley described it thus: "I make sure that the football board have the maximum financial resources and it is their job to get the best pound-for-pound value of those resources."

The theory might have seemed sound to Ashley but it was problematic. He faced huge mistrust on Tyneside that had started with the club's treatment of Kevin Keegan in the 2008/09 relegation season. The wrong people had been given positions of power, not least Joe Kinnear – appointed twice by Ashley despite the reservations of those who worked at the club. It was also difficult, at times, to work out exactly what it was that Ashley actually thought constituted success.

In one breath he would speak of building a future at Newcastle. He admitted his investment in the club meant that they were "wedded" to each other for the foreseeable future. But in a candid interview with the *Daily Mirror* in 2016 he admitted he regretted ever buying the club. "To get a football club to be the best it can be, you have to get the sun, the moons and the stars to align perfectly," he sighed.

The club had achieved some things on Ashley's watch. An off-the-field restructure meant the club's finances were much more manageable. Ashley was owed £129m by the club – a figure increased by a £33m loan in the summer of the 2016/17 season. That debt is owed to Ashley himself, which saves the club from paying millions in interest. For context, the club paid the bank £8m in interest in 2008 – just less than the amount they spent on recruiting Dwight Gayle.

Ashley had stuck his neck out and gambled that retaining key players, and not allowing a fire sale in the aftermath of the 2009 relegation would constitute a successful season. There was also the fifth-placed campaign in 2012. Those who met him speak with frustration about his time at Newcastle: they insist he is likeable and that his aims for the club are genuine. They say he has been let down by taking bad decisions at the start of his time in charge, which has seen him rowing against the tide ever since.

All of that was very difficult to square with the Newcastle of 2015: bruised, desperate, alienated and completely unsustainable. Ashley was aware of brewing supporter rebellion. He had been told to stay away from the Tottenham match that supporters boycotted, and reacted with dismay. Advised on that night in London that it was time to re-assert himself and actually speak to the fans to placate, he demurred.

There was no love lost with the media, who had criticised his mistakes. In Keith Bishop, a PR advisor whose other work was with celebrity clients, he had a man to help him deal with public relations. Surely speaking directly to disgruntled supporters would only make it worse?

By that sunny day in May, it felt unsustainable. Ashley had not said a word about Newcastle in the six years that had followed a brief statement following relegation in 2009. He was told that setting out what was to come next might rally the supporters. It was clear something had to change.

Sky Sports man David Craig is one of the few who has been able get close to the owner himself. The West Ham match was to be televised on Sky: it made sense for Ashley to speak on the channel that paid so much for coverage. He agreed to talk. In the stadium, as Ashley appeared on screens in the concourse, there was silence. It was an important moment.

Sky's first question: "First and foremost, I've got to ask, how disappointed are you to find Newcastle in this position?"

Ashley looked nervous. Certainly tense. "I can't have really imagined it since Christmas. I... probably didn't anticipate we would be anywhere near this situation. After the last couple of weeks I'm still a little bit shocked by where we find ourselves today."

"Who is responsible for it? Is it a collective responsibility? Or does it stop at your door?"

He responded, without blinking. "My door," he said. Would he invest if the club went down? "I will continue the policy of investing in the football club."

Ashley prompts another question, and is asked about what happens next if they stay up. "The only positive is we have the club on a very sound financial footing so we are able to spend relatively, and punch above our weight now with the current financial situation the club finds itself in."

Ashley is asked where Newcastle would be if he hadn't taken

over. "Financially, not as strong. But I'll add to that, it isn't good enough. It's not good having a horse and cart scenario. We may have the cart, financially, but we now need to bolt the horse on. And we're going to."

Then comes the bombshell. What is your ambition for Newcastle? "It's now going to be definitely to win something. And by the way, I shan't be selling it until I do."

He's asked to clarify. "Not for any price." Ashley is asked if there's a message to the supporters. "From this day forth, we'll be making our own luck."

On that day, Newcastle didn't need it. The supporters were galvanised by the relegation threat: the atmosphere missing for much of the season returned, and a fine 2-0 win secured Premier League football.

The second goal, gloriously, was supplied by Jonas Gutierrez – who had gone through chemotherapy for testicular cancer earlier in the year. His wild celebration came with a gesture towards the directors' box at the way he felt he had been treated by the club after his diagnosis. That conflict would spill out in an illuminating industrial tribunal the following year, which Gutierrez won.

Even among the celebrations, Gutierrez's gesture was a reminder of the rancour that laid beneath it.

***

UNTIL January of the 2016/17 season, Benitez not only had no contact with Ashley, he would have argued it wasn't necessary.

Benitez's plans for January had begun months before the summer transfer window ended. Regular meetings with Lee Charnley had kept a check on targets. Money had been generated from the Moussa Sissoko sale: the assumption that would be made available for January seemed a fair one.

The idea, according to those with knowledge of prior discussions, was simple. If things had gone to plan Newcastle would have brought in three Premier League players on loan, with a permanent deal teed up if they were promoted. The most prominent names mentioned were Andros Townsend, the Crystal Palace winger; Fabian Delph, the Manchester City midfielder; and Ruben Loftus-Cheek, the precocious Chelsea playmaker. Benitez – seeking to keep the club pushing forwards – believed that signing those three would not only copper-bottom promotion, but it would also mean that the following summer's work to prepare for the Premier League would be nearly complete.

Even before things got complicated, Benitez and Charnley would have anticipated bumps along the way. The impact of the huge TV deal on Premier League finances was to inflate the market. A £7m loan fee for six months' football would have seemed like an incredible deal a couple of years before: now even top-flight clubs with modest means could turn that kind of cash down in an instant. It made the market much more treacherous.

What Newcastle certainly didn't need was the return of internal politics – but that was what they got.

Benitez would argue that he is not a political operator. He does not buy the idea that he enjoys the jousting that comes behind the scenes. He says he is a tracksuit manager: a man who plots on the pitch, and whose strategies are about sporting success rather than consolidating power. Sometimes, he'd say, the battle arrives at your door.

Benitez anticipated his Newcastle would be active in January. With the Africa Cup of Nations set to take Mo Diame, Christian Atsu and Chancel Mbemba from him and now Shelvey's absence to contend with, he felt the club needed to react to support the ongoing promotion bid. He already felt that the club had entered the season one winger short. His feeling was that the squad needed to be supplemented with a wide player who could add creativity to the squad in a crucial January period.

Perhaps, to the outsider, it looked like Newcastle were hoarding footballers. They had cover in most positions, sat top of the Championship and were managing any injuries that they encountered. But Benitez saw the chance to strike out again in January, to add players using funds available and double down their advantage in terms of squad strength.

The recruitment remit had shifted. Newcastle still needed players for the Championship but, top of the division and with aspirations of playing Premier League football again, they had to occupy a unique space in January. To buy players who would be good enough for the top tier but prepared to drop into the Championship for five months would require recruitment skill, finance and a smart use of contacts.

The summer market was tougher than expected so no favours were expected in January. Still, Benitez felt confident that he could make a difference.

Buying from the Continent might have been an option. Another was to assess which players might be unsettled at not playing in the Premier League – and a discreet trawl of that market threw up some interesting names. Townsend, who had left on sparkling terms with Benitez, seemed unhappy at the way his move to Crystal Palace had unfolded. His relationship with Alan Pardew had not been good; his Selhurst Park successor, Sam Allardyce, seemed to harbour similar reservations. Benitez, in particular, saw this as a huge opportunity for Newcastle. Signing Townsend would recalibrate expectations in the squad and send an emphatic message to their rivals and Newcastle's own supporters. Charnley was urged to get the deal done.

This theory was a bit of an anathema to Newcastle, whose approach previously had been to buy when they needed to. January is acknowledged as a tough market to do business in and, 12 months previously, they had forked out a premium for reinforcements, largely because they felt they had no choice.

Wherever they turned, that premium was going to be a problem. Graham Carr had recommended Genk midfielder Wilfred Ndidi to the board. He was 20, rated at £15m and possessed the drive and determination that would make him a natural fit for the Premier League. A deal was always going to be impossible. Money and the player's own desperation to play immediately in the top flight meant a transfer was never a serious possibility.

As the month wore on, it became more fraught. The net was cast wider. The assumption of money to spend meant that names were being looked at. Everton's James McCarthy, another midfielder of international calibre, was the perfect Benitez buy. Technically gifted but also capable of the industry that Benitez wants from a midfielder, he felt like a perfect capture. Again, there were signals that the player would welcome a move north. But preliminary enquiries amounted to nothing.

They were not the only names being circulated. England internationals Tom Cleverley, of Everton, and Manchester City's Delph both illustrated the kind of quality that Benitez was looking to import. Neither would be cheap but if the idea was to fast-track potential summer signings, the logic seemed sound. That none were moving close to fruition raised concerns for Benitez.

So, too, did the lack of fluency in some of Newcastle's performances. Defeats against Sheffield Wednesday on Boxing Day and struggling Blackburn on January 2 were sandwiched by a win over Nottingham Forest that was not as straightforward as the 3-1 scoreline suggested. Shorn of the suspended Shelvey, Newcastle were showing signs of vulnerability. Benitez had picked up on these early warnings. He was hopeful of recruiting and pressed for resolutions but there was little sign of a breakthrough.

Insiders talked of a rising feeling of tension. Even a mooted loan move for Modou Barrow, a Gambian winger who could not break into Swansea's first team, did not materialise.

Benitez was sensing a shift in the dynamic and recalled young players Jamie Sterry from Coventry City and Sammy Ameobi from Bolton Wanderers. Neither had been considered ready for Newcastle's Championship squad at the start of the season but Benitez felt he had no choice with his options becoming stretched. Their recalls were a sign of problems.

When things got more drastic, Benitez even considered bringing Henri Saivet – the Bordeaux midfielder signed the previous January who had failed to make any impact despite a £5m price-tag – back to Newcastle. These looked like desperation measures not in-keeping with a manager as meticulous as Benitez.

Questions were beginning to emerge. Benitez held his counsel in public. Privately, it may have been a different matter. For once, the people that Benitez had plotted the resurgence of Newcastle with did not have the answers.

***

AT Birmingham City's St Andrew's ground in early January, Mike Ashley marked his return to Newcastle prominence. With the January transfer window a week old, it felt deliberate.

Ashley had met Benitez only once since joining Newcastle; a breezy, pleasant conversation in which they had got on well. Ashley's message to Charnley after that initial meeting was a confident one: give him the tools to do what he needs to do. But the vibes did not feel the same now that the warmth of the May sun had melted. The pair did not speak throughout a fraught January but they did not have to for problems to arise. Newcastle is the sort of club where others often do the talking for you.

Ashley's concerns about Newcastle's progress would not have been recognised by supporters, players or those who had witnessed the transformation in mood, results and the club's identity since he took over. But Ashley had illustrated over the years at Newcastle that he did not 'do' sentiment. In his mind, Benitez's popularity was only useful currency if the results were strong and the squad was not stagnating.

The owner started asking questions. Why had Benitez rested players for the first Blackburn game in the league in order to play them against Hull City in the EFL Cup? With Premier League football the priority, he did not understand that. To supporters who craved a club that took the knockout competitions seriously again, it felt like a return to relevance to see Benitez fielding almost a full-strength side in the cups.

One of the most unforgivable developments of the Ashley era had been the club confirming that the cup competitions were a secondary priority behind remaining in the Premier League. It was not just traditionalists and romantics who yearned for an end to the club's long run of more than half a century without a major trophy to end, who felt that was an outrage.

Benitez was practical about the EFL Cup. He said that promotion was the priority but he would judge the mood and pick a team to win. By reaching the quarter-finals Newcastle had positioned themselves well and his team for the Hull game was his strongest available. United lost that game on penalties and the league matches both before and afterwards. Ashley was not pleased.

Ashley also saw squad players signed in the summer who had not played, and questioned the idea of investing further money. Achraf Lazaar, the Moroccan defender, had barely featured after a move from Lazio. Daryl Murphy could not force his way past the strikers Newcastle already had, despite a seven-figure investment. Jesus Gamez, the veteran defender, was similarly lightly used. The team would need to be overhauled in the summer and selling 'dead wood' is tough. It did not make sense to add further to this group.

Ashley remained in contact with Carr, whose presence amid questions about recruitment was hardly a co-incidence. In the court of Ashley, the chief scout had always had his ear. The owner wanted him involved in decisions again. Given the fact Benitez had assurances his was the first and last word in transfers, that was going to be a big problem if enforced.

It felt telling that when he turned up at St Andrew's for an FA Cup third-round tie, he did not speak to Benitez. Carr was there, though, by Ashley's side. Perhaps the most important moment of that day was when the Newcastle manager handed in his team-sheet, which revealed several changes to the starting XI. Had he prioritised the cups over the league again, no doubt tensions would have ratcheted up a notch once more.

With Ashley occupying the no-man's land between front-line involvement and passing interest, it created a crippling confusion and paralysis at the club. It was left to those in charge to try and smooth the tensions that it created. It was an almost impossible situation for Charnley to work in.

Ashley, no doubt, would be unapologetic about the intervention. Newcastle's owner had quietly, and without much fuss, loaned the club an additional £33m to cover losses incurred by relegation. Effectively, this money funded the changes that Benitez was so keen to make. If Benitez was the architect, Ashley would have pointed out that he was the money man.

Quietly, those who had Ashley's ear also asked why Newcastle were second in the Championship after the talk in the summer of the club's complete resurgence. A story that appeared in the Sunday newspapers in the middle of January made some of these issues public, heightening the sense of tension in the North East. A 2-1 win at Griffin Park, the home of Brentford, was achieved in front of the watching Ashley. Among the revelations in the article were the fact the owner was demanding a return to the policy of recruiting players under the age of 26.

Griffin Park is tight and compact. You can barely move in the corridors there without bumping into people. Yet there was no direct contact between the owner and manager again that day.

Now the issues were in the public domain, Benitez would have to confront the issue. Having lost the war in Madrid, he would have to play things carefully.

***

THERE is an argument that the winning goal at Brentford on January 14 was the most important of Newcastle's season. It is a theory that deserves a wider audience.

There were more enthralling goals scored by Newcastle, bigger games that they competed in and more desperate situations that they extricated themselves from. But for what it symbolised, Daryl Murphy's header in the 79th minute of that game sent a message that surely ended the debate about the recruitment decisions Benitez had taken in the summer.

The Republic of Ireland striker had cut a slightly frustrated figure at the training ground. From time to time, Benitez would mention him – apropos of nothing – at his press conferences, praising his work ethic. Aleksandar Mitrovic's lack of game time was a bigger issue on Tyneside, given his reputation but Murphy – who had played regularly for Ipswich – was just as important to Benitez. Keeping him sharp was important. Murphy understood why others were preferred to him, even if he didn't always agree.

The signing of Murphy was the moment in the summer when Benitez was able to illustrate his complete control over player recruitment. It was not a move that others – most notably chief scout Carr – would ever have proposed. If Pardew, Carver or McClaren had asked for it, they would have been given short shrift. To Benitez, there was a cold, hard logic that far out-weighed the gamble of investing £3.5m in a player who would not appreciate in value.

Until January, the form of Dwight Gayle had meant that he was not required. But at Griffin Park, when Newcastle's top scorer dropped to the ground having aggravated a hamstring muscle, Murphy's opportunity arrived.

It was a strange game. Gayle's opening goal on 20 minutes was sensational – a surge into the box from the left and a terrific finish, high into Brentford's net. Newcastle had the ascendancy but Gayle's injury forced a reshuffle.

The hosts edged into the game and began to gain a foothold. Lasse Vibe levelled from close range early in the second half and Newcastle's fluency completely deserted them as Brentford laid seige to their goal in search of a winner.

Instead, it was Murphy who made the most emphatic statement of the day. Drifting into the Brentford box, he met Ayoze Perez's wonderful right-footed cross with a deft header. It was a critical goal. Newcastle moved back to the top of the table and Benitez's gamble on Murphy was beginning to reap rewards.

Benitez had bought him for his experience of the division: of his ability to influence games in ways that weren't always quite as pronounced as scoring the winning header. Vindicated during the run-in, he was asked why he signed Murphy.

"On the first day after I stayed I was told, 'You don't know the Championship.' Some said to me: 'Will Rafa be good enough,'" he explained.

"You need people in the Championship to manage [important] situations. In the 94th minute of a game, when you should keep the ball and not give the opposition a chance to play a long ball. Players with experience can help.

"You need a balance between young players, hungry with motivation, and those who can calm people."

The message was clear and simple. Benitez's calls were continuing to pay off.

That was the confusion of the cussed January transfer window. If Newcastle's manager had been given the tools, funds and free rein to do his job in the summer, it did not make sense for him to then run into a roadblock in January. His knowledge and experience was what Newcastle were investing in. It was essential that they continued to do that.

***

BENITEZ was perplexed and frustrated. But there was an important caveat: he did not want a war. There was to be no prodding of the nuclear option. He recognised things would be tense and strained. It was important they weren't inflamed more – both for the sake of the supporters and a dressing room that didn't need the distraction. Tyneside crackled with talk of an insurrection if Ashley's power play forced the manager out, but that was never a prospect that anyone on either side entertained. But it provided a crash course in the internal politics of the club.

If battle lines weren't quite being drawn, perhaps the power lines were. Chief scout Carr had spent the afternoon in the company of Ashley at Birmingham at the request of the owner. Benitez and Carr seemed to have a cordial relationship – the former, touchingly, sent the latter's family a Christmas hamper – but the chemistry at the club during the month changed. An element of suspicion stalked the club during January.

Like Ashley, Carr felt that some of the criticism levelled at him was unfair. He had been expected to leave in the summer but his close relationship with Ashley, forged during the days when he was bringing in exactly the type of player that the owner's business model relied on, was a protection.

Carr, the father of TV comedian Alan, lives in Northampton but his affection for his boyhood club is beyond doubt. He had been offered the chance to move to other clubs during his time at Newcastle but said no. He wanted Newcastle to be contenders in the Premier League again and despaired, at times, when the club seemed to go into battle with the people who wanted it to succeed.

Newcastle was his club: he hadn't wanted to leave in the summer. The strength of his relationship with the owner was an intriguing sub-plot to January. When his stock was really high, Newcastle appointed Kinnear as director of football and Carr was close to walking, having felt his own role was compromised. Ashley paid a personal visit to him to persuade him to step back from the brink.

This was not the 'constant presence' of the chairman that Benitez had felt at Real, but perhaps things were not quite as simple as he had first imagined. This was not the politics of the Bernabeu, but it was a distraction nonetheless. Other managers would have been cowed or outraged. Benitez went another way.

The win at Brentford bought Newcastle time. Benitez retained his hope that Townsend could be signed. They saw off Rotherham United 4-0 but, with injuries biting, Benitez fielded a young and inexperienced side at League One side Oxford United. The 10th youngest side ever fielded by the club, they lost 3-0 in what was nonetheless a humiliating blow in the FA Cup fourth round. Newcastle's team was lopsided and featured some young players pruned from the Academy who could not get in the under-23 side. There was a not-so subtle message underscoring the team selection, which included a number of graduates and boasted an average age of just 24: Newcastle required reinforcements.

Deadline day dissolved with Newcastle unable to broker the deal for Townsend that they had wanted. Charnley, under pressure from both sides, was looking for a loan but did not want to become tied into the expensive permanent deal Crystal Palace wanted. Benitez was left frustrated. Still, he was not in the mood for war. Peace in our Tyne, even if a warning was to follow an unsatisfactory 2-2 draw with QPR – played out in a stadium that felt full of dread. Rumours that Benitez would walk out – unfounded, even if his discontent was accurate – were an unwelcome backdrop to the match.

The team were poor. A last-minute Ciaran Clark own goal left

Newcastle second, again behind Brighton. Shelvey was back but there would be no fresh impetus. United would have to find improvements from within.

Ashley, obviously, was not in the mood to do interviews. Instead, this time it was Benitez's turn to appear live on Sky. Again, David Craig was the interrogator.

The Sky man got three questions. His first: "It's been a busy week for everybody, Newcastle chose not to strengthen in the window. With the benefit of hindsight and a result like tonight, is that a decision that you would like to revisit?"

Benitez's response was abrupt: "My decision was very clear. It was not my decision."

Sky followed it up. "It's not your decision [not] to bring in new players?"

Benitez reaffirmed: "It wasn't my decision."

Sky's man tried again. "Would you have liked to bring in those players?"

Benitez's third – and final – answer. "It wasn't my decision. So I said what I wanted, what I needed, what the team needed and that's it."

It felt like a warning shot but Benitez stressed the need for focus both inside the dressing room and outside of it. It was a blow – a confusing, surprising development – but there could be no excuses brokered for what was to come.

Benitez had articulated his frustration. He had wanted support from the boardroom. Now he needed support from the stands.

15. Inspiring A Movement

Sparking A New Fan Culture At Newcastle

"Until Rafa I wasn't happy"

Newcastle United supporter's banner, 2016

IN 2014, Newcastle United were blindsided by a very modern sort of rebellion.

It began on social media and leapt into the mainstream. 'Pardew Out' – a collection of 50 and 100 disaffected fans connected by social media application WhatsApp – was what happens when a club becomes so divorced from its supporters that they feel they have no choice but to protest. And watching it spread like a virus among a fanbase accused of apathy was a compelling pastime during their two years of prodding Newcastle's belligerent hierarchy.

Pardew Out was born in late 2014 and it's aim was simple: to force the club to sack manager Alan Pardew. They felt he was out of his depth, unambitious and leading the club in the wrong direction – and they resolved to do something about it.

Shape-shifting, contentious, creative and unapologetic, they were the first shot in a St James' Park spring that nearly swept Pardew out of office.

There had been rebel yells before. Supporter protest was not a new phenomenon. But what was fresh was the idea that the energy of online discontent could be harnessed to try and force the club into changing an approach which, they felt, was a case of death by a thousand cuts.

In essence they were just a group of Newcastle fans armed with mobile phones, a Twitter account, a slick website and some eye-catching posters. But very briefly they managed to harness their energy and collective desire to see Newcastle change, and managed to dominate the nation's football headlines.

"We just got fed up of where the club was going," one of the leading members told me. They decided on anonymity at the time because they felt they would be branded super-fans with an agenda. The message, they said, was more important.

"It was just complete discontent. About the things that Pardew said – that we couldn't compete with Southampton, of the football that we were watching, of the club's lack of ambition, of its happiness to appoint a man like Pardew who had been a League One manager before he got the job. We felt it needed shaking up."

I met the group a few times back in 2015. They laughed about what they said was a David vs Goliath fight – the might of Sports Direct owner Mike Ashley and his team of PR men and lawyers against their collective knowledge. They were ordinary fans with full-time jobs from different backgrounds. They saw this as 'Them against Us'. Even though they were Magpies fans, 'them' was Newcastle United.

It was blunt, a single issue protest that they wanted to take from the Internet to the mainstream. The objective was to force the club's hand on Pardew by making as much noise as they could. It was simple, direct and a reflection of just how alienated a big section of Newcastle fans felt at the time.

Their tactics were fairly simple. "I think to an extent we played games with the media a bit. We knew that we needed to give the photographers a good picture so we'd tell them in advance where we were standing, what we were going to be holding. I think we made ourselves look bigger than we were at first, and then it gained momentum from there."

They gained further coverage for their eye-catching banners. One, unfurled at Swansea City, read:

'LLWDLLLWWLWLLLLLLWLLDDLD – not a Welsh town, our form in 2014'.

They knew that not everyone approved. Some fellow supporters felt they were making Newcastle fans look entitled. Pundits said that focusing on Pardew was wrong, given the fact that he'd managed to keep the club safely in mid-table. That was rather the point of the exercise.

"A lot of people said that there had been worse times at Newcastle United but we didn't really buy that argument. If you grew up during the days of Kevin Keegan and Sir Bobby Robson, why not aspire to get back to that? What was the point of a club just existing to exist?"

Pardew clung on. Newcastle had given him an eight-year contract and he retained their support. They bristled at being told what to do. But the group had made a big enough noise to achieve a breakthrough of sorts. They had made things awkward: forced the club to at least acknowledge the issues they talked about.

"We felt that the club regained its focus a bit. When Steve McClaren was appointed he got money. We forced the issue. Maybe none of that would have happened without us," they say now.

Later, they switched focus to Mike Ashley's ownership. They were invited to meet Lee Charnley during the relegation battle, a summit that was set up but never took place. One of their worries was that Newcastle's fanbase would stop caring. That apathy would take over and the club's biggest asset – its support – would end up walking away. Their controversial intervention changed that. The energy – good, bad, desperate – was back.

"When Rafa Benitez got the job, we just felt this surge of satisfaction. He was everything we'd been urging the club to go for back in the Pardew days. He is a world-class manager. In an instant all the things we'd said would happen if they did that – getting the fans behind the club – happened." Their campaign lies dormant these days. They hope there will never be a need to fire it up again.

There is an energy about Newcastle fans that revealed itself in the Pardew Out campaign. Rafa Benitez wanted it channelled into something positive.

***

ALEX HURST writes and podcasts for long-running fanzine *True Faith*. If you want to take the pulse of Newcastle United, this is a pretty good place to start.

During the days before Benitez, the editorials written by former editor, Michael Martin, were such howls of discontent that they sometimes came with a health warning in case they boiled the blood too much. Little broke the cycle of despair. Until Benitez's arrival, that is.

In an instant, the mood lifted. The rallying calls to protest morphed into something else. The man had to be backed. Benitez had joined because of the club's supporters – Martin and Hurst used the podcast as a platform to rally fans to recreate the noise that had gone silent during the dog days.

Even they underestimated the enthusiasm created by Benitez's first few months. If Pardew Out went viral, the next supporter movement took on a life of its own.

"'Gallowgate Flags' happened sort of by accident," Hurst recalls. "It started with a call to get people to move to the Gallowgate to create an 'end' where Newcastle fans, who wanted to create an atmosphere, could all congregate.

"A lot of people hadn't renewed their season tickets because the deadline was March and (Steve) McClaren was still here. Once that happens, there's no going back, you have to buy a new season ticket. So we said: 'Let's move to the Gallowgate.'"

Martin felt Newcastle could aspire to even more. The ultras of Italy and supportive collectives of Germany were an inspiration and aspiration. Could the 'Newcastle end' be supplemented by visual displays to rival grounds across Europe?

Hurst, on a placement in America, finding himself a bit bored, offered to take the lead. A fundraising Kickstarter campaign was launched with the idea of raising a couple of thousand pounds to purchase a flag or two.

Newcastle had been relegated, but Benitez was confirmed for the Championship by then. Season tickets were selling. People were ready to invest in the club again. Within two days the campaign was at £2,000. By the end of the week it was £5,000. After a slightly chaotic meeting at the Strawberry Pub outside St James' Park, the fund was at £9,000. This was big. It was also different.

"We were not going to be a protest group, no matter what happened. Individually, people could say what they wanted. Gallowgate Flags needed a relationship with the club. We'd seen the club try to engage with people before and get their fingers burned. Our school of thought was to support the team, whatever happens.

"We were not a fans' group. We'll not get involved with protest. We go to support. We won't be shouting and swearing at Vurnon Anita if he gets done at right-back. That's not what we're about."

They bought 500 flags with the money. Before the first home game of the season, Newcastle unlocked St James' Park and 20 fans spent six-and-a-half hours unfurling the flags and placing them around the ground. Newcastle United's head of marketing and communications, Lee Marshall, was one of them. They left at 11pm and returned at 10am the following morning to finish the job.

Benitez heard about it and told the club he wanted to find a way to support it. He spoke publicly about it: communicated a message of support. There was a video on the website. He asked that Newcastle give it everything it needed to succeed.

"Rafa was the catalyst for it all. The fact that he'd put his trust and faith in a club in the second tier of English football made us think we had to do something," Hurst says.

"Yeah, season-ticket sales were great. People were buying tickets but we felt we had to do something more as a fanbase. It's time for us to give something back."

It looked sensational. Under the bright, Tyneside sun the ground was transformed. The pictures went around the world: *AS* in Spain picked it up. *Gazzetta Dello Sport* featured one of the pictures.

Newcastle lost 2-1 to Huddersfield. "The atmosphere was bouncing before kick-off – but then it died. A few people had a go at us, saying it'd take more than flags to win the league. It was frustrating. It was a bit unsustainable," Hurst remembers.

Like most modern football grounds in England, sometimes the atmosphere does not match expectations. Newcastle were on their way to recording the second-highest second-tier average attendance in history but the enthusiasm for Benitez sometimes met with the cold, hard reality of a teak-tough league. Fans didn't turn up until close to kick-off, which meant the crowd took a while to get going. Some felt there was too much expectancy on the team to win. That way danger lies: Benitez was always aware that the 'Rafalution' hype might create an expectation of blowing teams away. That's why the flags idea appealed so much and was encouraged.

The job of changing the feel of the stadium – of creating a Borussia Dortmund-by-the-Tyne – was not going to happen overnight. They decided to become more targeted: to do the displays when the team needed them. Martin spoke of changing the culture, of getting fans to actively support, rather than thinking that just turning up was enough.

In those early days of February, the Gallowgate Flags moment to affect change arrived. After the January transfer window, Benitez's terse post-match interview and his call to arms, there was a feeling that the season could go either way. One national newspaper screamed out on the day that followed the 2-2 draw against QPR that Benitez was "on the brink". Benitez's long-term future felt more uncertain, his project threatened. Ashley did not reach out and it was left to Charnley to try and calm everything down. Tyneside fretted.

So Hurst clicked open the WhatsApp group again. "The QPR game had been so flat. I think people will look back at the season and forget what a critical point that was. Huddersfield were threatening us a bit. You could sense the tension and sometimes, Newcastle is a difficult place to play when it's like that."

An impromptu display, concentrated in the corner, was arranged. The Gallowgate fans assembled an hour before kick-off. Noise rose. This was support in its truest form.

"I think the atmosphere that day was one of the best of the season. It wasn't a great game but it was really supportive. There was a real noise," states Hurst.

Newcastle won 1-0. Derby, now managed by Steve McClaren, pressed late on but could not break United down. It was a gutsy win. A Benitez win.

"The fact that he is here represents something so different from Mike Ashley. We're a football club again," he said.

"What we had before was a club that existed to exist. His presence in the city has changed that. He was on Spain's biggest radio station the week before the season started. Newcastle managers aren't a big deal in Spain usually.

"He's such an asset to the city, the region, the football club. This feels like a big opportunity for Newcastle. It's not just on the club or the players, the fanbase has to rise to that as well."

By February 4, Newcastle were top again. Getting by with a little help from their friends.

16. Rafa Benitez Gets To Work

A Day In The Life Of His Training Ground

"You could try the same thing with a different group of players and it wouldn't work. But this was a group who wanted to learn"

Rafa Benitez, May 2017

A SHORT, sharp blast of Rafa Benitez's whistle. Newcastle United's training ground in February: sandblasted by a bitter coastal wind that rolls in from the North Sea.

The second week of the second month of the year brings cold, grey days and the work must seem attritional. Professional football can be a gilded cage at times but there is nothing glamorous about days like these, when Benitez has assembled his squad to work in the business end of the season. It is easy to bring intensity in

August and September, when the challenge is new and the body fresh. It is the middle of February, when limbs are aching, minds are fatigued and the desire of Championship opponents to land the division's prize catch remains undimmed that Newcastle must maintain their intensity.

That is the way Benitez views it. The consistency he talked about on those relaxed, long summer days before the season began and he was setting out his stall for the campaign to come was not a message to placate supporters or inspire his squad. He meant it – and it is when the cameras are off, the players are confronting the challenges of the seventh month of the season and his demands are the same that Newcastle will prove themselves.

The word is consistency over the course of a difficult season, of course, but Benitez's English teams have an unerring tendency to finish well. Liverpool and Chelsea's seasons ended with a flourish: two FA Cups, one Champions League and a Europa League are testament to a training programme designed to deliver at pressure points in the campaign.

Benitez's plan was always put together with an eye on the long game. The philosophy was communicated clearly and precisely to the players early on and if they were ever in any doubt, they are not now. He has stuck to exactly the same principles that were set out on the first day of pre-season.

It's no bad thing. They know what is expected from them, day in and day out. They must show intensity and a "winning mentality" in every minute of every training session. In or out of favour, on the back of a winning run, a goalscoring streak or a collection of clean sheets: none of that matters. Come to work to win or your position in the team is under threat. Benitez is no dictator. There are no screaming matches or public dressing downs for his players. He wants them to come to work with a smile on their face and to enjoy what they do. But he is absolutely firm about the need to maintain their levels of work.

So in February, when the grey skies hover above the chilly Benton neighbourhood that houses Newcastle's training ground, he is looking for signs of who has hit the wall and who has lasted the pace. These are the days in the season when Benitez gauges who he can rely on as the big games start to roll in.

A typical Rafa Benitez training session lasts between an hour and 90 minutes. Over the course of the season he will stick to the 80/20 philosophy – the idea that you should spend 80 per cent of your time training with the ball and the remaining 20 per cent on conditioning and fitness.

The players warm up for the first 10 minutes of the session and then go into short, sharp technical drills. These concentrate on crisp passing, sharpening the reflexes and honing technique. One of the drills Benitez has used involves all 20 members of the squad, which sees a pitch divided into four sections and is contested between two teams of 10. Regardless of which team you're on, a maximum of four touches are allowed in each zone before the ball has to be moved into the next zone. That lasts for around 10 demanding minutes and the emphasis is on retaining possession of the ball for your team.

Ask the players what they think about that and they'll give it a ringing endorsement. It hones mind and technique – the idea is that if you can last the pace in that exercise you can make good decisions in games, too, retaining your ability to think clearly while also sharpening technique in the middle of a match.

There are principles that Benitez sticks to. But passing and shooting drills are tailored to improve the areas of the game that Benitez feels his players need to be better at. His coaching team are reactive, assessing data fed to them by unobtrusive GPS and heart-rate monitors, to tinker with the way training is laid out.

Benitez, along with assistant coach 'Paco' Moreno, has a degree in physical therapy and he likes to teach. That thirst for improvement is sated on the training field.

One quick example. When Benitez first took over, he saw things in Aleksandar Mitrovic's game that needed to be tinkered with. Mitrovic, to his credit, drafted in Allan Russell, a specialist forwards coach whose firm, Superior Striker, specialises in improving off-the-ball movement and anticipation through statistics and analysis. Russell works with Romelu Lukaku, Saido Berahino, Andre Gray – players on an upward curve but who require refinement. Mitrovic had the raw talent and enthusiasm but, despite the eight-figure fee Newcastle paid for him, he remained a rough diamond. Hours and hours were put into improving him, making him understand the craft of striking rather than relying on impressive but untapped potential. He may not have scored the goals Dwight Gayle did, but Benitez recognised the improvement in his all-round game.

The players, even in the middle of a gruelling Championship marathon, enjoyed the sessions. They were receptive and reactive. The joy of working with Benitez did not dim. He loved the fact that all of them wanted to learn: their hunger remained, even when fatigue crept in.

"We have a way to do things," Benitez explains.

"Our methodology is working with the ball all the time, so they enjoy that, and changing the exercises but keeping the same objective – things that we have done for many years. For some of these players they are new things," he said.

The analysts were busier than they had been for years. Short clips and longer show reels – the ones that Cristiano Ronaldo snorted at when it landed in his email inbox – were devoured. Matt Ritchie and Isaac Hayden asked for more information. The players hunched over iPads and took in every morsel.

"We have the analysis department and clips for every player, as well as the team. We try to give them feedback in terms of what they do. They appreciate that and are keen to learn and improve so that it creates a very good environment," Benitez added.

Newcastle were not Real Madrid; the Championship was not the Champions League. But before the season started, his resolve was always clear: treat the two competitions the same. Prepare and work in exactly the same way at Newcastle United than he had done in his previous roles.

"In terms of how you coach, how you train, how you organise things, you have to do things in the way you did before because you were successful," Benitez said.

"I was obviously talking with people [before the season started], learning about the division and the mentality of the players and the kind of players you can bring in, all these things.

"People sometimes say, 'This is a player good for the Championship, not for the Premier League', but what you have to do is make sure you achieve what we want to go up," he said.

Having taken the temperature of the group before the season kicked-off, he had confidence. The background checks, the desire to generate a positive mentality; all of it seemed to be paying off. That was not knocked by defeats in the early weeks of the season.

"I had confidence in the team," he repeated. In pre-season he had liked what he had seen from the group. They listened, they learned and they were prepared to work. Perfect, he'd thought. His hunch had been proved right in the autumn and there was evidence of it every day at the training ground. Weariness in previous seasons had been the gateway drug to a lack of professionalism at Newcastle. Not this year.

***

BENITEZ played the long game in the Championship but Francisco de Miguel Moreno – or Paco – was entrusted with managing the 'microcycle', piecing together a programme for the blocks of one or two weeks that would determine how Newcastle would approach individual runs of fixtures.

By the time Newcastle had edged past Derby to regain top spot, the pundits were ready to start calling off the chase. Benitez could not have disagreed more. Newcastle had 15 games to play in 85 days – an average of one every five days. From past experience, attacking the back-end of seasons attempting to compete in Europe and domestically with some of Europe's biggest clubs, he knew how gruelling that could prove.

Benitez felt maintaining mental focus was even more difficult in the Championship than in the Champions League because of the "monotony" of continuous league games. There were none of the new sights, smells and challenges of criss-crossing Europe, which maintained mental sharpness among the elite. These were hard yards across cities and towns where they wanted to grind Newcastle's noses into the dirt. To avoid that, they would have to prepare properly. Paco's microcycles were going to have to be perfect if Newcastle were going to maintain their control of the promotion race.

Below Newcastle and Brighton, maintaining their own impressive effort, there were a group of teams enjoying riding in the slipstream. Jaap Stam's Reading were within touching distance. Leeds United, rebuilt under Garry Monk, were making noises about challenging and backing up those sentiments with eye-catching wins. David Wagner's Huddersfield Town had emerged as the clearest threat to the Championship's duopoly, surviving an autumn dip in form to burst into 2017 in excellent form. Their intensity was causing problems for Championship teams and they had managed to avoid injuries for much of that winter.

Ever a student of the game, Benitez enjoyed sitting down with the analysts to look at the way his Championship rivals played. The tactics weren't always as subtle as the ones he'd had to pit himself against in Italy, Spain and in European competition but there were fresh ideas in England's second tier.

"We have been changing little things in different games as we go along," Benitez said in February. The system remained solid but he was tweaking it for different challenges. In the middle of the month, he started liaising with Moreno on the work that they would have to put in for a run of three games against their nearest challengers which would surely define their season.

After beating Derby, Newcastle's next games were Aston Villa at St James' Park, a reunion with Wolves at Molineux that would prove every bit as fractious as their first meeting, and a game against lowly but unpredictable Bristol City. The fixture list then sent Newcastle to eventual play-off finalists Huddersfield Town and Reading in the first week of March – two away games that had taken on increasing relevance, given the jobs done by their respective managers.

FA Cup wins for Newcastle and Brighton in January had thrown an extra challenge into the mix – arguably the biggest of the season. The original game between the pair had to be rescheduled and Newcastle were dismayed by the EFL's decision to pencil it in early spring. Despite a request by Newcastle to reconsider, United would be sent to the south coast on February 28, a third game in a week against the teams around them. The EFL's edict could only be challenged if both teams wanted it to be reconsidered: Brighton, perhaps sensing a chance to exploit Newcastle's workload, were happy to play on the date the league had given. It was not ideal. A new problem to be solved.

***

THE analysis room at Newcastle's training ground was one of the places Benitez felt needed to be re-decorated. There used to be two signs up there which were intended to keep the players' focus. One read: 'It's not about blame, we're all accountable.' Another, affixed above a wood panel door, read: 'Be an intelligent team. Learn when to do the right thing at the right time.'

To be brutally honest, it felt a bit drab. But for Benitez's team, the 45 minutes spent dissecting the opposition were some of the most critical of the week. Brightening it up, making it an environment where players come to listen: these were summer tweaks that had to reap rewards in this part of the season.

It is Antonio Gomez Perez who heads the analysis department. It is his responsibility to collate the information about opponents, to splice the footage into manageable chunks and to disseminate it to the players. There are times when he and Benitez talk long into the afternoons about the footage that arrives from Opta Pro or a team of scouts who monitor the matches in the flesh. Even with every second of every match played in the Championship available at the push of a button, Newcastle have eyeballs on the matches their opponents are playing.

For Perez, the relentlessness of the schedule suited his tireless nature. He tells me that Benitez likes to have every morsel of information that he thinks is relevant, but that he has the complete faith of the manager in what he thinks will help the team.

"It is nice to know that the manager has that trust in you. We are a team – we win together and we also lose together. But my job is to make sure that the players know everything they need to know," he says.

It is a big job. Knowledge is important but overloading players comes with a risk. There can be a paralysis in analysis and modern-day football is much more open to the idea that there can be an edge to be gained from working well with statistics.

At Championship rivals Brentford, they employ a team of university-educated mathematicians with no background in professional football to pore over footage that will give them the edge in both recruitment and match analysis.

For Perez, the overriding feeling of the season is that Newcastle first need to stand up to the physical challenge. Then they need to get smart.

"The Newcastle experience is something new for us," he admits. "It has been a fascinating season for us because this league is not something that we are used to. So we watch a different team in the Championship and think: 'Oh, they do that this way.' You are having to look at different systems, different ways that teams play.

"And the games come every two or three days so it is very intense. The players may have to cope with one system one fixture and then something completely different the next. That is not always the way in other leagues where teams may play in a similar way," he says.

Benitez concurred. The Championship was a learning curve. "Everything is different. Tactics must be different. We were up against direct teams, passing teams, three at the back, five at the back. Eight at the back, even.

"I have had to adapt to different tactics. Every week, twice a week, you have to adapt and change. And you do not have a lot of time to prepare the way you really want."

That piled the pressure on his assistant. He works with a team of analysts, some of whom were already at the club. "They are very good. Their knowledge is important," he says.

Three games that arch over February and March will define Perez's work. The fixture list has laid its traps – Benitez's team believe that preparation will protect them.

***

MOLINEUX has hardly raised itself from a slumber this season but the home of Wolverhampton Wanderers has a frenzied feel when Newcastle come to town.

Wolves is a grand club, sat in the middle of the city like Newcastle. A Chinese-backed takeover in the summer that preceded the season was promoted as a game-changer but their early win at St James' Park proved a false dawn. Management was confused, their direction baffling. Walter Zenga, who ruffled Magpie feathers in the first meeting, is long gone – replaced by Paul Lambert. Newcastle needed to win. Huddersfield's victory over QPR – a third in succession, following impressive defeats of Brighton and Leeds – narrowed the gap to third to four points. The Seagulls had responded to their loss with victory over Burton Albion. The top two was tightening.

Newcastle had to dig deep. Perez's away-day formula was to make the team compact and difficult to beat. Jamaal Lascelles was immense alongside Ciaran Clark: United defended stoutly.

The bad blood that remained between the two teams was barely far from surfacing. The ill-will that followed the contentious Jonjo Shelvey suspension earlier in the season gave the game an added, ugly edge, and hair-trigger forward Mitrovic played his part.

Already booked, he went in late on Wolves goalkeeper Carl Ikeme, studs raised. Molineux howled for a second yellow card. Craig Pawson, the referee, hesitated. Mitrovic survived and scored just before half-time. It was the only goal but the home crowd did not forget. They sang loudly about Shelvey throughout.

Mitrovic was withdrawn at half-time for his own "protection". It was a performance laced with ill-discipline from the striker but Benitez felt the referee was not helping him. Again, the feeling that Newcastle were being targeted was the implication.

The mood in the dressing room afterwards was buoyant. Newcastle had become a band of brothers over the course of a difficult season. The squad had started their own WhatsApp group, which helped build team spirit and togetherness – the 21st century version of the pub visits that used to cement the bonds between players. Given the way Wolves had reacted back in September, this was one of the sweetest wins of the season for them. That it had been earned with backs against the wall made it more satisfying.

After the game, a pumped-up Lascelles shot to the defence of his colleague. "It was terrible what happened to him last time. It should never have happened. Jonjo is not that type of person." Lascelles said Shelvey had "embarrassed" Wolves. Benitez picked up the thread in the post-match interview, saying The FA should look into the crowd for their anti-Shelvey chants.

It was perhaps not one of the most impressive things he said that year but it was a sign of him throwing a protective embrace around a group showing signs of resolve when it mattered.

It was certainly required. A week later they played Bristol City in a game that should have provided Newcastle with one of their more straightforward wins of the year. But two-down at half-time and shocked by visitors who arrived prepared to put Newcastle on the back foot, Benitez's men were reeling. Huddersfield – away at Barnsley – were ahead. Their supporters sang that they were 'coming' for Newcastle and the threat was serious. The lead was down to a point at 3.45pm.

Newcastle rallied. Fury and unity from the terraces created a fearsome noise. They pulled it back to 2-2. A Barnsley equaliser at Oakwell meant the gap remained at four points. It was an insurance policy as they headed into their three most dangerous assignments of the season.

***

BENITEZ was always confident that Newcastle would go up. He always talked in terms of the club progressing and being a Premier League side in a year's time. Every single meeting that he held about transfers that followed January was with an eye on the challenge in the top flight that was to come.

It was reassuring to hear him talk that way when the mics were off or to learn from those close to him that he was making those plans, even if the public message was different. It was designed to reinforce the idea that nothing had been settled at any point of the season. Benitez is an engaging, interesting commentator but his press conferences became predictable. The idea that Newcastle still had work to do was an obvious one, but he repeated it time and time again.

The confidence that he exhibited in private was not representative of a devil-may-care attitude. There was potential for damage to be inflicted in the hat-trick of games against their nearest rivals, and Benitez even had an alternative message planned if Newcastle somehow slipped out of the top two after the away games against Brighton, Huddersfield and Reading. He knew that ground could be made up in April: the month which contained seven games and, which he believed was going to be key to deciding what mattered in the Championship.

Behind the scenes, Benitez had redrawn his own points target. Huddersfield's doughty chase of the top-two positions meant that he now believed that 90 points might not be enough to take Newcastle back into the Premier League. Ninety-two might be the magic number required: another 22 points. Newcastle, back down to second after the Bristol City slip-up, were facing their most pressing set of questions yet.

***

CHRIS HUGHTON was the accidental Newcastle manager. A man who arrived at the same time as the posse of advisers, board members and technical directors who would come to be derided in one supporter's banner as Ashley's 'Cockney Mafia'.

Unlike the likes of Jeff Vetere – vice-president in charge of player recruitment – and Dennis Wise, executive director of football, Hughton endured. He was appointed by Wise to help shore up the defence during the days of Kevin Keegan and slipped effortlessly into the background.

Hughton's career is a storied and interesting one. He was the first mixed-race footballer to play for the Republic of Ireland. He was an elegant defender in his day, who played close to 300 games for Tottenham, a club he'd also coached at. But in Newcastle he wouldn't have been picked out of a line-up when he first joined the coaching staff.

There was one afternoon, called to support a Show Racism the Red Card event at Newcastle's stadium, where reporters crowded around Shaka Hislop to hear stories about the 1996 'Entertainers' and Hughton was left to his own devices with a cup of coffee. You would never have guessed back then that he would have such a transformative effect on Newcastle – or Brighton. It just did not feel in Hughton's nature to force the issue.

He remained a hero with many Newcastle fans for the way that he handled the club in the aftermath of their last damaging relegation, but now he was proving a hindrance. Brighton & Hove Albion are a team moulded in the image of their manager – hard working, effective and possessing of a never-say-die attitude which had lifted them above pre-season favourites Newcastle. Benitez's side were the best away team in the division; Hughton's the best at home. It was a critical match.

Newcastle, again, were backed by a sold-out allocation. A match switched because of FA Cup commitments was also now on Sky, but it remained a hot ticket.

It did not begin well. Brighton applied pressure, which Newcastle had expected them to do. But there was a glitch in the robust defence that had served United so well at Wolves and in their away days. Benitez, agitated, leapt from the dug-out in the third minute. He made a habit of that: it was rare for him to spend long on the padded seats. The temptation to be out of his seat, cajoling and analysing, was always too much for Benitez to stand.

Hughton had urged his team to hit the channels and move the ball quickly. He wanted to replicate the high-intensity start that had troubled Newcastle against Bristol City – and it was working. Twice Karl Darlow was forced into outstanding saves, beating away Bruno's long-range effort before Sam Baldock's looping shot was tipped over.

Benitez bellowed from the touchline for his midfielders to show more composure. Things were not going as they'd planned it. Momentum needed to be disrupted. Jack Colback had been picked to break up the play, but the march of the blue and white shirts was troubling.

Then there was another reason for Benitez's ire – a familiar one. Fourteen minutes had passed when a corner was dropped into the penalty area. Ciaran Clark and Glenn Murray wrestled in the area, referee Bobby Madley pointed to the spot. Confusion before the cheers: few in the sold-out AMEX Stadium seemed to realise what had been given. There was nothing uncertain about Murray's penalty – his drive was low and to the right of Darlow. Benitez fumed about the decision.

Newcastle absorbed the shock and began to assert themselves. The game-plan hatched on Benton began to take effect. Newcastle looked the more likely for the rest of the half. Christian Atsu was playing with pace and poise down Brighton's right-hand side and angled a shot that tested David Stockdale. In the dressing room at the interval Benitez asked for calm. Newcastle would have their chances: they just had to be in the right place to take them.

The players, again, spoke to each other. "We said that we need to push on," Mo Diame said. They had stood off too much. With Atsu flying on the wing, surely it would not be long.

It had the feel of 'one of those nights'. Paul Dummett cleared off the line. Newcastle's let-off gave them an opportunity but they lacked a ruthless edge. Stockdale coughed up possession, incredibly, on the edge of his own box with a slack pass. Yoan Gouffran, the man dragged in from the cold by Benitez, dallied. Stockdale's recovery save left Newcastle sick. The goalkeeper's right boot deflected Gouffran's shot and forced Benitez's hand. Daryl Murphy, the saviour at Brentford, was summoned from the bench.

His impact was instant. A strong header forced Stockdale to tip behind for a corner and, from the next phase of manic, madcap play Newcastle, utterly improbably, had a foothold in the match. The corner was cleared towards Atsu, who shaped to execute a first-time volley.

His shot was screwed wide. The AMEX howled its derision but Diame stood in the ball's path, six yards away from goal. It rolled off his right boot and looped into the night air. The stadium gasped as the ball dipped at an angle. It was dropping under the crossbar and Brighton defender Fikayo Tomori reacted, jumping to try and deflect it over. But the dip was impossible: 81 minutes gone and Newcastle had their leveller.

Around the ground, there was a beat. The ball was in the back of the net but there was silence in the stadium, as if no-one could believe the goal. Then a guttural roar from the away end. A huge moment in Newcastle's season.

"I got lucky," Diame said. An understatement. Newcastle's hard work had paid off: making their own fortune again.

Benitez sensed the shift in fortune and sent for Ayoze Perez. The forward's contribution had been fitful over the course of the season but Benitez likes Perez a lot. He has quick feet and is capable of playing at speed. With Dwight Gayle still out injured, he was the best hope that Newcastle had for making the most of their speed. Gouffran, the man surprisingly picked as the lone striker, was the man to make way.

It was an inspirational piece of in-game management. Newcastle continued to press and with 60 seconds left on the clock their remodelled team used their pace and poise to prise open Brighton's defence. Matt Ritchie hit a terrific long-range ball over the top of Brighton's defence, which Atsu controlled deftly. One touch and then a second were enough to put Bruno on the back foot and he rolled the ball into Perez's path for the winner.

The substitute had timed his run perfectly. With chaos around him, his first-touch finish was precision personified. "Cool and composed," Benitez said afterwards. "We were lucky but we earned our luck," he added. He strode to the centre of the pitch to seek out his players, shaking each of them by the hand.

Hughton, in the opposite corner, was "sickened". He retained his composure and congratulated Benitez with the grace that Newcastle fans would expect. But his team had been hit with a classic, away-day sucker punch.

Newcastle's players were ecstatic in the dressing room but Benitez urged focus. Huddersfield was just a few days away.

***

IF Brighton was Newcastle making their own luck, Huddersfield was the fulfilment of Benitez's best-laid tactical trap. It was, surely, his most satisfying evening of the campaign.

Huddersfield boss David Wagner had revelled in his team's identity as a "small dog" attempting to take a bite out of the big boys and now his side would have the opportunity to rip a chunk from the division's biggest. It was high noon for the high press from West Yorkshire.

When Benitez said he would ideally have had more time to plan for the matches, this was what he meant. Newcastle's fitness and performance had been excellent throughout the season – a consequence of having a young, hungry side. They ran tests midway through March and found that in 75 per cent of the matches they'd played, Newcastle had the edge over their opponents when it came to 'high-intensity sprints'. That meant they were winning the 50/50 balls and forcing the issue with their opponents.

But there was little that you could do about mental fatigue. And for a game like the one against Huddersfield, where there was a blueprint to follow, that could be problematic.

Benitez wanted his team to walk the tightrope between making sure they took no unnecessary risks while also going for a win that would put a sizeable dent in Huddersfield's own aspirations. It was Stratego all over again. Defend doughtily and pounce when the opportunity arises. Classic Benitez tactics.

Huddersfield crackled that night. Terriers fans came in expectation of their team pressing and pushing Newcastle, and the result was a pulsating contest. Crucially, it was the visitors who drew first blood. This time, Newcastle benefited from a marginal decision: Matt Ritchie the man felled in the penalty area, and then emphatically converting.

Wagner, banished to the stands, must have been pleased with the response. Huddersfield moved through the gears but Newcastle pressed them back. Newcastle retained their shape, despite Huddersfield's best attempts at disruption. Every single player did the job that had been asked of them, faultlessly.

Why was this significant? This was Newcastle, a club that 12 months previously had seen Georginio Wijnaldum go rogue at Chelsea and Jamaal Lascelles complain that "no-one gives a f*ck". When Lascelles had challenged the dressing room, no-one had responded at first. That team of individuals, looking to lay the blame elsewhere, could not have been further from this collective effort.

Huddersfield were applying the pressure but Newcastle were bobbing and weaving. This was Benitez's own rope-a-dope: a black and white version of Muhammad Ali's famous strategy to absorb the pressure of George Foreman before unleashing his own sucker punch. On half-time that jab arrived when Daryl Murphy – starting this time – latched on to a mistake by goalkeeper Danny Ward and dispatched from a tight angle. He hared to the advertising hoarding and bellowed into the pitchside mic. Newcastle were decisively in command.

Huddersfield remained dangerous. Elias Kachunga was pushed by Jonjo Shelvey and Aaron Mooy converted the 72nd-minute penalty. Newcastle redoubled their defensive effort. The crowd grew more intense. Benitez sent for Gayle. He scored late, stealing a goal when Ward was caught out with a high, 'Hail Mary' clearance. Gayle motioned with his arms for the crowd to calm down. Two wins out of two: the most resounding of Benitez's tactical successes.

***

IN the end, Newcastle emerged from their three-match examination with seven points, a goalless draw at Reading ending that run of testing fixtures. Newcastle could – and should – have won in Berkshire, but tired limbs dulled their edge. Huddersfield had beaten Aston Villa and so the lead was cut. Still, Benitez was delighted with the way the hat-trick of big games had gone. Promotion and the Premier League felt close. Publicly, Benitez counselled caution. They were wise words.

17. A Nasty Surprise

Dealing With Setbacks – And A New Kind Of Pressure

"Physically, the team is fine but when we get close to the box sometimes, you can see that anxiety is a problem. We must solve that"

Rafa Benitez, April 2017

AFTER victory at Huddersfield, it looked like the final games of the season would be a victory lap. Newcastle had reasserted themselves but the black and white promotion juggernaut had barely moved into second gear before genuine promotion rivals appeared in the rear view mirror. It was a testament to the difficulty of the Championship challenge that the response of the promotion pretenders was so impressive.

Benitez on the back foot? It had not been the case so far. But in the final weeks of the season, he had to fashion a positive response in adversity.

For the outsiders, it was no doubt an enthralling prospect. Brighton's resilience – hewn from the character of their manager and a squad that had played together for consecutive seasons – saw them bounce back from the Newcastle defeat and a debilitating reverse at Nottingham Forest with two straight wins. Huddersfield proved again that there was substance to David Wagner's work by winning against Aston Villa and then away to Brentford. Benitez had a race again.

Privately, the manager upgraded the points total he felt would be required once more. March was motoring on and the references he'd made to April's important fixture schedule were becoming more and more frequent.

Benitez, the meticulous planner, had divided the season into sets of matches when the fixture list came out. The microcycles that Newcastle would work to on the training ground would be devised around these sets. Even back then April stuck out to him: 21 points to play for, seven matches and the potential to decide every crucial issue to Newcastle's season. Even when they team were flying in November, managing the risks around this month was on Benitez's mind.

He certainly mentioned it enough publicly. In press conferences Benitez was asked if the bulk of Newcastle's work had been done. He would namecheck April frequently.

The month was a minor obsession and the work done the previous summer – the building he had tried to continue in January – was carried out with the belief that the team that accelerated into the penultimate month of the season would be the one that won promotion. Newcastle's new approach to fitness and medicine had ensured that injuries were managed but – as 'Paco' Moreno had said back in the autumn months – they were inevitable when players had such a heavy workload. Isaac Hayden, crucial in midfield, missed a long spell of games. Dwight Gayle suffered a hamstring relapse. Jamaal Lascelles was playing through the pain barrier with a double hernia. Newcastle's squad was being tested but not stretched: they had the players to cope.

Suspensions, too, were a concern for Benitez. Matt Ritchie's volatility had left him teetering on the brink of another suspension for yellow cards accrued.

This was where the likes of Jesus Gamez, Grant Hanley and Daryl Murphy – all bit-part players for long periods – would come in handy. Gamez played at Reading, Murphy at Huddersfield and Hanley at Birmingham as Benitez made the most of his squad. They had cost several million to buy but they helped Newcastle to win points: it seemed like prescient summer logic. A few had questioned him at the time but Benitez remembered those first days at Newcastle with no fit left-back to pick. A similar error could have been fatal to promotion hopes in the home straight.

This attitude was absolutely key to understanding Benitez's approach and the way he viewed Newcastle's priorities in the Championship season. He was meticulous and prepared for everything, two characteristics which helped Newcastle to achieve their aims. But it also laid him open to charges of being risk averse and, occasionally, too defensive.

Sky Sports' Football League anchor Scott Minto is one of the most erudite and under-rated pundits on television. A former footballer who played for Benfica and Chelsea, he had zig-zagged the country during the course of the season, watching the division's best go to toe-to-toe. Interestingly, he had also seen at first hand the way Benitez operates when the pair worked together on Sky's *Revista De La Liga* programme.

There were many guests who would stroll into the Isleworth studio a few hours before kick-off, make pleasant chat and react off-the-cuff to what they had seen from whatever Spain's match of the day was that they were watching. Benitez – who was then the

Liverpool manager, with all the work that entailed – would come in armed with a clipboard and pad.

"He was absolutely meticulous and methodical," Minto tells me. "Even when we had a 0-0, we didn't have a problem with Rafa picking out the talking points. His analysis of the games was absolutely razor-sharp. He would sit with a clipboard and pad looking at how the game was unfolding, and his ability to digest what was going on was pretty impressive.

"Rafa would see the overall direction of the game and work out why it was happening virtually instantly – he's incredibly tactically astute. When people talk about a football brain, he's got one.

"I think Rafa is at that stage in his career where he's accrued so much experience that is being added to what is a natural gift anyway. You work with a lot of people in football and he's pretty unique in the way he's able to analyse things quickly, which is probably a reason why he's been so successful."

The theory ran that Newcastle should have been well clear by this stage but their unexpected slips – especially at home, especially now the promotion race was contracting – were troubling some anxious fans. As there had been for much of the season, there was some debate about whether Benitez's resistance to playing two recognised strikers was too cautious against teams that came to Tyneside to defend.

Those who said that perhaps need to be reminded of Benitez playing chess or Stratego with his brother in the garden in Spain. There were certain inalienable principles of Benitez's philosophy – the belief in managing an opponent's threat was one of them.

An obsession with "balance" was another. Benitez was proud of the fact Newcastle were top of both the goalscoring and clean sheet tables. "We don't concede many and we score goals, so this is a good combination," he said. It was a mantra he repeated whenever anyone asked about his preference for playing with one, rather than two strikers.

He had homespun wisdom that drilled right to the heart of his philosophy. He spoke of the "short blanket" problem on many occasions – the idea that, if he shaped the team with more forwards it would be the equivalent of pulling a blanket up to his neck, only to reveal his toes to the cold.

On mentality, he talked early in the season about Newcastle now being the "head of the mouse, not the tail of the lion. When you are in the Premier League, you are the tail," he said, indicating that United approached the season with the idea they were a small fish in a big pond the year before. "Some people are happy with that, some prefer to be the head of the mouse."

Benitez was telling his players to get used to being the big game in the Championship safari.

It was interesting to hear a neutral perspective, and Minto's theory was that Newcastle had adapted pretty well to being favourites for the division, given all that they had to overcome in those first months of the season. He felt that Benitez's tactics and methodology were sound – as their position in the table illustrated. But it was perhaps a style that would come together more completely in the top flight against opposition with a different mentality to the second-tier sides Newcastle were welcoming to St James' Park.

"It is perhaps a counter-attacking strategy," he said. "Rafa's style is better suited to playing teams that are a bit more on the front foot and there will be more of that if Manchester City, Chelsea and Liverpool are playing at St James' Park.

"You could see how well they did away from home when Rafa has employed his system and it's worked to a tee. The Huddersfield win was a perfect example of that."

Having banked those away-day points in West Yorkshire, Hampshire and Berkshire, the Magpies' promotion odds narrowed to 1/500. Even those who had witnessed Newcastle's Premier League title collapse in 1996 might have been forgiven for believing the race was nearly run.

The visit of Fulham to St James' Park was the nastiest of surprises. It prompted a fresh set of problems to find solutions from.

***

WHEN Benitez was a younger manager, he would endure sleepless nights after defeats. Working for Real Madrid, it did not happen that often. But when it did, he would bristle at the criticism and drive himself to distraction with the idea that someone – and something – had failed.

When he left the confines of the Bernabeu's talent factory, he lost more but also learned more. When he took charge of Real Madrid Castilla – the 'B' team that plays in the third tier of Spanish football – it was a more difficult job. Defeat came more regularly at Real Valladolid, Osasuna and Extremadura – his next three managerial jobs.

"I started my career as a coach in the Real Madrid Academy," Benitez explained in an interview he conducted with the club at the end of the season.

"We were winning maybe 80 per cent of the games. You didn't lose too much but then, when you leave and you realise that the other teams are quite strong and you can lose, that's when you start learning. It's quite difficult, but that is the way.

"You have to lose some games to realise how important it is to do things well – to concentrate on the little details, the small things that can change a game.

"You have to have balance. If you lose a game you are disappointed but, at the same time, what the people – your players especially and your staff – expect from you is a reaction, a positive reaction, a solution. You have to be calm, keep your composure and then analyse what is going on to give a solution or an idea at least, and they can then follow this idea."

That coolness was going to prove important as Newcastle dealt with the setbacks down the home straight. That began at home against Slavisa Jokanovic's side on March 11 in one of most chastening afternoons of Newcastle's season.

Fulham were the side that had slapped any complacency out of Newcastle when the season began. Now it was not so much that United had again lost the return fixture, although the defeat reawakened dormant fears that the team would conspire to throw away their advantage at the top of the Championship. It was the way Fulham played: a young, mobile side that oozed with poise, attacking intent and a fearlessness that had not been evident in Newcastle's home performances for so long.

Fulham's former Leeds United midfielder, Tom Cairney, a player that Newcastle had enquired about in December and had subsequently baulked at the £20m asking price, posted an early warning of what the visitors were about to do with a wonderful swirling effort from 25 yards after 15 minutes.

We waited for the United response. The idea that they could not respond to setbacks was no longer a valid one, given the way they had hit back at Brighton or even earlier in the season against Norwich. But instead of conjuring a riposte, they began to make mistakes. Benitez, again agitated on the touchline, looked as frustrated as he had all season. He had urged caution before the game: not to give Fulham a foothold in the match. Now they had more than that, and the danger they posed was increasing with every minute of the match.

There was an irony underscoring Fulham's footballing lesson. It arrived 12 months to the day that Newcastle announced Benitez as manager. So much had happened in the interim but here Newcastle were, playing as if they were the same collection of malcontents that he had inherited from Steve McClaren. The group chemistry, the hunger to learn, the willingness to absorb Benitez's lessons – all swept away by the red shirts of their fleet-footed opposition. Tyneside unpredictability strikes again.

There was an eye-catching turn from Ryan Sessegnon, Fulham's 16-year-old left-back. He scored twice in the second half before the hour, sweeping into the Newcastle box on both occasions to capitalise on mistakes.

Murphy's excellent goal 14 minutes from time was not enough to prompt a fightback. In truth, United deserved no more on a day when pretensions that promotion was already won were turned on their head.

Newcastle were shaken. Huddersfield played again on the Friday and the gap to third could be reduced to three points if they defeated relegation-threatened Bristol City.

Benitez would take this setback on the chin. For all that analysis had been key to their surge to the top of the table, they had not picked up any signs of the calamity to come in training. There were some days that mystified even this veteran manager: this was one of them.

In the days before the game, the team-talk had focused on the need to restrict Fulham's control of the game. They'd analysed the Cottagers' play and worked out that they'd had 70 per cent of the ball in their three previous games. Newcastle needed to be smart, to match their intensity and to try and get their midfield on the ball more. But they could do none of that. Nothing worked: Benitez's half-time tweaks were rendered ineffective by the mistake that handed Fulham their second goal on 51 minutes.

These were the sort of days when the manager of Newcastle required the broad shoulders that his predecessors, perhaps, did not have. When the days were sunny, the results were positive and the praise easy, anyone could have done the job. But defeat to Fulham brought edginess. Benitez talked of "anxiety" around the team when they played at home.

It was their fifth defeat at St James' Park. There was a problem that required a solution. It says much about the way Benitez worked that it was the last reverse they suffered on their own patch in 2016/17. In the meantime, the anxiety was rising. There were yet more solutions to find.

***

THERE are some times that a response can be conjured on the training pitch. Now Benitez asked for a feel of the mood on Tyneside. It felt edgy: tension that was about more than just Newcastle's eroded lead at the top. There was a historical dimension to worries that the pressure was getting to Benitez's young group.

The response was two-pronged. To Huddersfield, he attempted to apply some pressure to their apparently fearless players by making references to the anxiety that would rise in West Yorkshire as they approached the final weeks of the season. Benitez always felt that they would have to deal with the challenge of confronting the magnitude of what they were about to achieve. The question was whether their fearlessness would survive those final weeks.

Raising that publicly was a deliberate attempt to change the Championship agenda. Wagner didn't bite. "A relegation fight is pressure. What we have at the minute is only excitement and it is very enjoyable what we are doing," he said. But Huddersfield's bandwagon was to be derailed in spectacular fashion with a 4-0 defeat at Bristol City. Two key players picked up injuries. It was the fork in the road for Town's automatic promotion prospects.

It calmed some anxieties, but Newcastle's response was lacklustre. Benitez fielded a team at Birmingham City without Jonjo Shelvey, who had been laid low by a sickness bug. Blues were there for the taking but United could only draw 0-0. Brighton did not win either but Huddersfield lived to fight another day. The edginess also endured.

Benitez felt it was time to take on some of the questions that Newcastle fans had head-on. He had an open invitation from the local newspaper, *The Chronicle,* to answer the queries that supporters had raised in a mid-season survey, but he'd demurred in January when the questions were first posed.

Now, with eight games remaining and nerves fraying, it seemed like a more appropriate time to get his message out there. It was an international break with no club football to play. Benitez would often agree to talk or to address fans' questions in that break, aware that there was a vacuum of news in the days without a Newcastle game.

Before the start of the season, in the summer months when transfer rumours run wild, he'd done the same with *The Chronicle* in June. It brought the focus back to him. In the hermetically sealed world of football, it was a different approach but he appreciated the way the modern media worked. For a club that had banned the local newspapers in the mistaken belief that they could wrestle back control of the agenda by strangling the source of information, it was some sea change.

Benitez's approach was to confront the accusation that his football was safety-first head-on. To questions of caution, he mounted a robust defence. It was about balance, he communicated. He pointed out that they had scored the most goals in the division, and had conceded the fewest.

"I would ask people to consider that we are top of the table," he said. "What we are doing is working."

The idea that he would change direction in the middle of the season came as a surprise to him. Newcastle had not started with two up front all year. That had changed once – the progress-through-chaos denouement against Norwich, when Newcastle threw caution to the wind and caught the Canaries on the hop. That 4-3 victory did not feel like justification to Benitez to suddenly take unnecessary risks.

He recycled an analogy he had used before – that of the "short blanket". If he played two strikers and reverted to a 4-4-2 formation it would risk the balance of his side, he claimed. If he pulled the blanket up to make his team stronger up front, he risked weakening his midfield or defence with the short blanket.

It was an interesting take. Benitez had been compared to Kevin Keegan and Sir Bobby Robson but his philosophy on football was a world away from that of 'the Entertainers'. They would attack teams with the implicit understanding that it would make them vulnerable. Benitez did not think that would work.

It said so much about the way Benitez had fostered alliances, built credibility and worked on his relationship with the supporters that they were so willing to listen. It also spoke of a man who knew he was answerable to the supporters. For all that he'd achieved – for all that he knew they trusted him – he was prepared to communicate his reasons. He would not be bowed by accusations of caution, but he knew he owed them that. The honesty was appreciated and trust reciprocated. It felt open. At a club where the communication lines had been opened again, Benitez's willingness to engage on the criticism, as well as the optimism marked a sea change in approach.

And why wouldn't he do that? Results had not been outstanding since Huddersfield but the Spaniard was confident in his methods. The consistency he had spoken of in the summer had endured two bad results at the start of the season. It could endure here.

His justification felt fair. At every juncture of the season, Benitez wanted to point out that there was a methodology that had gone into his team selection, system and tactics. There was a warmth about the man, but a steely, cold logic that underpinned his approach to the Championship challenge. It would not change.

"It would be a mistake to think that we are always able to run at teams and get the victory because of the quality in our squad. There are many other teams in this division with great strength and quality," he said.

"Some people could look at our game plan away at Huddersfield and say it was too cautious, and that we should be pressing from the first minute to get the win. But our approach to sit back and let them come at us was the best tactic for that particular game. Football management means considering every opponent and every game in isolation, and deciding what is the best way to win each game."

The confidence was also a message to the players. Wigan and Burton were the next two home assignments. Two relegation-threatened sides. They would be contests decided by Newcastle's ability to open up robust defences.

"I was always talking about April as a crucial month," Benitez said after the season finished.

"Still, I always had confidence. It would be hard, it would be difficult but we would do it."

18. Credit Where It's Due

Why Newcastle Knew They Were On A Hiding To Nothing

"If we win promotion, people will say: 'It's only because of the money'"

Rafa Benitez, April 2017

A FEW days before the 2016/17 season – this long, marathon campaign – concluded, Rafa Benitez was asked what he made of the term 'Rafalution'.

It is a shorthand phrase for the huge changes made on his watch but it's not a Newcastle original. It was swiped from Liverpool, where Benitez turned Gerard Houllier's underachievers into a club that secured Europe's biggest prize in his first season in charge. In six years at Anfield, his personnel, policy and philosophy turned around the Reds.

At Newcastle, he was required to do so much more than just make the club competitive. He had to recalibrate a club that had lost its purpose. The 'Rafalution' was about much more than the things that went on at the training ground alone.

The club liked the phrase, too. From a marketing perspective, it certainly gave them the opportunity to draw a line under what had gone before.

"I'm really pleased with the support of the fans," he said. "But I think that I don't like to talk about the 'Rafalution', I think that it has been more an evolution of everything.

"By that I mean in terms of the approach, because sometimes when you have a shock it's how you react. Relegation means that we had to react. We had to start doing things in another way, and that's what we have done in almost every department of the club. It has been good in the end because we have been successful."

Benitez has always shied away from the idea that it was him who was responsible for everything that was good at the club. In his eyes, he was an enabler and facilitator for a lot of the changes that happened. He set the tone from the top, but it was the kit man, the analysts, the secretaries, the security guards and the ground staff who responded to the changes that he brought in.

This was partly true, although it was Benitez who added the substance to the rhetoric. Previous managers had spoken about engaging the fans: it was Benitez who turned up at supporter meetings, unexpectedly, or at community events. It was the manager, too, who proved that he cared about the Academy side by watching both of their end-of-season play-off games, when other bosses might have been forgiven for rewarding the efforts of the campaign with a well-earned break.

His actions did help the club. For a long time they had felt cowed by the mistrust. Good initiatives that club staff pioneered or came up with were shelved or flew under the radar because of the poor relations between Newcastle and supporters and the city institutions they had alienated. For example, Newcastle's match tickets were among the cheapest of the top clubs. It did not get the praise it deserved.

The irony – given his occasional reticence to take unnecessary risks on the pitch – was that Benitez had encouraged the club to take a few more risks off the field. Long before the season ended, they had started to talk to supporter groups about the prospect of a singing section to be congregated in the corner of Gallowgate. A previous section had been broken up; the club said to enable them to build a section just for families. Supporters thought it was because of anti-Mike Ashley chants.

Other little things began to crop up. Corporate ties were improved. At the dramatic Norwich City home match, some of the region's biggest businesses were being entertained – firms who might have shied away from association with the club in previous years. The Newcastle United Supporters' Trust was re-admitted to the club's Fans' Forum meetings, having been banned for three years over the way they had communicated at a previous summit. Local businesses were back in the fold, and they started to work more closely with the council again. The club's media team were also given access to film more behind-the-scenes footage to share with the supporters. Benitez's appointment and attitude created a more open club.

Benitez was perhaps being modest when he said it, but he honestly felt that the capacity for the club to act properly was there before he arrived. He just gave it a little push. "It's not fair to say that it was a low base when we came in, because the structure and the organisation were fine," he says.

"Then you have to improve maybe in some departments about how you make decisions, or whether you take risks, or not, little things like this.

"The majority of the departments, they were doing well. So it's just to fix two or three things to be sure that they click together."

The lesson of Benitez had been learned right at the top. When Lee Charnley was asked what would happen if the manager left – and West Ham had maintained a friendly enough relationship with him after his rejection to make those fears something to take seriously – he admitted that the club could not go back to the head-coach days. It had taught those in charge of the club that there was an importance about appointing a figure with the right experience, cache and personality to turn the club around.

That, surely, was the Rafalution in a nutshell. The Mike Ashley era had seen the club ignore overtures from supporters, media and experts that they needed to change direction. But Benitez's appointment had put them right. Even without Benitez, the implication is that Newcastle would never go back to the small-time way of thinking that preceded him. The realisation that a manager of cache, charisma and possessing of broad shoulders was required will be part of his legacy, wherever Newcastle go from here. That is some change to inspire.

***

THERE was a title to win and a promotion to earn but Benitez knew even that would not be enough for some who had peered in on Newcastle's progress in the 2016/17 season.

A hiding to nothing, he would later agree. Newcastle's budget, support and his own presence on the touchline meant that they were expected to win every single match they lined up in.

They went into April's big games on the verge of clinching promotion but Benitez was still bristling. He had won Manager of the Month just once – in November. His name rarely came up when people talked about the Championship's Manager of the Season. If pundits talked about the job Benitez did, it was more along the lines of him capitalising on the advantages at his disposal.

Granted, Newcastle's wage budget was beyond most of their

rivals. So, too, was their ambition. But they were not the only team who had invested to try and procure promotion. Aston Villa had spent more and were marooned in mid-table. Wolves were fighting a relegation battle despite significant Chinese investment. The shortcomings of other teams who had been relegated from the Premier League, and had failed to bounce back in previous seasons was proof that it required significant skill to make a success of a potential promotion campaign.

"I don't know if we have received the credit we deserve," he admitted. "I have been on both sides of the fence – at teams with money, and teams with no money. I used to get upset at things like this. Now what we must do is give everything.

"People say: 'Oh, but you have money.' That does not matter. You just have to go out and win.

"Yes, we are pleased to win games, when we score goals and don't concede. Here, to achieve what we are trying to achieve is quite complicated. Every year, you see the teams that are relegated and not all of them do well.

"Everyone will have their opinion. If we win promotion and they say, 'It was only because of the money' then so be it. Before the season starts, everyone has an opinion. But the only one that is right is the one that is proved correct."

Perhaps the way Newcastle listed in the final weeks of the season illustrated the job he had done picking a way through the unpredictability of the Championship.

Two home wins followed the international break. The edgy 2-1 defeat of Wigan was unremarkable but for the fact that Huddersfield slipped up again, caught with a sucker-punch by Burton in the 96th minute. Newcastle looked to be on the brink.

Burton then visited St James' Park in a match tinged with farce. Their opponents were obdurate but benefited from an outrageous piece of refereeing. Having awarded Newcastle a penalty after Dwight Gayle was barged to the ground, Keith Stroud was then guilty of one of the most contentious decisions of this or any season. Newcastle converted the spot-kick but Gayle crept into the box. Stroud blew his whistle. St James' Park anticipated a re-take but the referee gave a foul against the home side, to the astonishment of the coaching team.

It was one of the most incredible decisions ever given at Newcastle. On the touchline, Benitez remonstrated furiously with the fourth official Tony Harrington. Mikel Antia thrust an iPad with a clarification of the rules in front of Harrington. The farce continued for seven minutes – and then again in the tunnel as the players sought out Stroud to hear more.

Luckily for the integrity of the division, Ritchie's second-half goal separated the teams but it further soured Benitez's opinion of the officials. By this point there was a distinct feeling from the Newcastle manager's camp that his team was battling the referees as much as he was opponents.

Newcastle's rhythm was disrupted. They went to Sheffield Wednesday on the following Saturday. Benitez paid a personal visit to the Hillsborough memorial a few hours before kick-off, laying a wreath in memory of the 96 victims of the 1989 disaster on behalf of himself and his family.

Newcastle were to kick-off late due to TV commitments. Huddersfield were beaten at Nottingham Forest and the promotion prize was within touching distance. But an error-strewn display saw them lose to a motivated Owls with play-off aspirations.

An Easter resurrection remained on the cards: a win against Leeds on Good Friday would mean promotion guaranteed by Monday. But Newcastle conspired to throw away two points to Garry Monk's side, dominating throughout before Chris Wood pounced with the visitors' only clear-cut opportunity of the second half in the fifth minute of injury-time. It winded Newcastle. The gap was back down to eight points and chasing Huddersfield had a game in hand.

Benitez counselled consistency on the training ground but it felt as if the pressure was beginning to asphyxiate some of the players who had swaggered during autumn. Newcastle were accused of stumbling towards the line. The new question posed of their manager was whether finishing second in the division would constitute a failure or let-down. Given that Benitez already felt like he was on a hiding to nothing with those critics outside the club, it felt like a loaded question.

Newcastle's mission from the moment they started to assemble plans for the Championship was to achieve promotion. There were no extra payments for winning the title, just a flat £7.1m on offer for every team that competed in the division. Newcastle were the most televised club in the division but that was only worth another £700,000.

Those stark figures told their own story. Sunderland's risible effort in the Premier League in the same season would reap £93.4m in prize money payments. Newcastle had a £40m parachute payment and the overdraft facility underwritten by Mike Ashley, but the inescapable truth was that failing to win promotion would mean everything changed at St James' Park.

Benitez would not countenance or contemplate missing out on promotion but contingency plans had to be drawn up, and Newcastle would have looked like a very different kind of club if they had missed out on bouncing back at the first time of asking.

Fans of the club would do best to look away when you contemplate the potential consequences. Jonjo Shelvey, Dwight Gayle and Matt Ritchie would all have been made available for sale immediately, the necessary way to cut the wage bill and bring in revenues that would be missing any of the Premier League television revenue bonanza.

Others would have followed them through the door, replaced by free agents or players prepared to be paid significantly less to drag down what would have been seen as unmanageable costs. The club's accounts, released in April, hinted at as much and came with a stark warning from Lee Charnley.

A redrawing of the club's financial landscape would surely have meant the end of Benitez, too. He may have had two years left of a three-year contract but the questions would have been just as much about Newcastle being able to afford him as they were about the Spaniard staying. Having been persuaded to take a chance on a world-class manager, Ashley's response to failure to win promotion at the first time of asking would surely have been to revert to type – whatever the best intentions of the board. Good money after bad? More likely pare everything back and face the consequences of fighting in the Championship on a more level financial playing field.

Charnley, who had been part of the reason that Ashley agreed to back Benitez, would have known that his job would have been at risk. Others might have felt a similar squeeze. The foundations laid by Benitez might well have been bulldozed. It was a stark, nightmare scenario that few wanted to acknowledge. At a time when potential Premier League rivals were expanding – ambition, their stadiums and their global reach – it would have set Newcastle back decades.

The flip side was Newcastle in the Premier League. Charnley flew to China in April to talk commercial opportunities and ways the club could grow its brand. Benitez's Liverpool connection means he is one of the names that resonates in the Asian market. There was a renewed interest in Newcastle. Players had already been identified; agents spoken to. Benitez seemed enthused about what could be achieved with the city behind him in a division where he felt more at home. Promotion would not just mean more money, it would give Newcastle the opportunity to fulfil the potential project he had sold the club in the summer.

When Benitez talked about the pressure on his shoulders, this was what he was talking about. Newcastle's sliding doors moment:

the right move now opened up a future which was brighter than it had been for years. Newcastle had missed opportunities to grow before, but none would have ushered in as dramatic a change as not gaining promotion from the Championship. It was a pressure that was never vocalised by anyone at Newcastle officially, but it lingered over those final, fraught weeks of the season. They knew what was at stake.

It perhaps explains why Benitez remained untroubled about not winning the league – even when his players, like Isaac Hayden, were admitting that finishing behind Brighton would leave a "sour taste" in the mind.

Aware of the issues that finishing out of the top two would lead to, Benitez disagreed. "Second place would be fine with me," he said. Many had pin-pointed Chris Hughton's ability to re-energise Brighton after the play-off failure the season before as one of his biggest achievements. But Benitez saw that failure differently: he felt that it had helped bond the Seagulls. His team had been brought together in six summer weeks; Brighton knew the league and were utilising that experience in the final few games.

It got much nervier after the team served up its worst performance of the season at Portman Road against an Ipswich Town team they had pulverised at St James' Park. Newcastle's display was as anaemic as any under Benitez. The players were tetchy and the mood was replicated in the away end.

"The worst away atmosphere of the season," Alex Hurst, the Gallowgate Flags co-founder said, matter-of-factly. The Championship was testing Newcastle again. Huddersfield kicked-off against Derby 30 minutes after the final whistle at Portman Road with the potential to cut the cushion at the top to five points – a gap that would be shaved further if they won their game in hand.

"It is still in our hands," Benitez insisted afterwards. He was convinced that they still had enough. He retained the calm exterior of a man untroubled by the worry that was sweeping his fanbase.

Perhaps underneath there was a measure of panic but, if there was, he was not showing it.

All Newcastle could do was wait on the result in the East Midlands. Colin Quaner's goal on nine minutes handed Huddersfield the advantage but then something funny happened. Benitez had warned the pressure would mount on David Wagner's promotion hopefuls and, at Pride Park, they retreated into their shell. Huddersfield's season had been a story of fearlessness but they looked cowed by the potential of reeling Newcastle in.

In the away end the fans chanted about "coming for Newcastle" again but the team were not playing like it. They hung on. It looked as if they had survived but in the 88th minute of normal time, Jacob Butterfield's deflected shot breached Danny Ward's doughty resistance. Huddersfield looked broken: they knew the game was up. Form and fearlessness had deserted them at the last and the shift in momentum played into Newcastle's hands.

A further slip at home to Fulham confirmed that Huddersfield were running on empty. Newcastle needed only a win at home to Preston North End to go up – and the Monday victory arrived, somewhat nervily at first, but emphatically in the end. Ayoze Perez broke the Lilywhites' resistance early before the team were pegged back by a goal from Jordan Hugill, a Teessider who relished spoiling Newcastle's party. Nerves returned; Hayden soothed them with a wonderful interception and run that teed up Christian Atsu on the stroke of half-time.

The relief was tangible. Matt Ritchie converted a penalty, Perez added a fourth. St James' Park was euphoric. In the dressing room afterwards, Trap music rung out. The 2009/10 vintage had listened to *Dignity* by Deacon Blue before and after most games – a possibly tongue-in-cheek reference to what they had restored to the club. This was different: a younger group who had allowed DeAndre Yedlin to take over the stereo. Aleksandar Mitrovic added to the chaos by soaking Benitez with Champagne. The smiles and joy reflected the job well done. Benitez was asked in the post-match press conference about his own future. "You never know in football," he answered, diplomatically. Even that could not dim the celebrations. Newcastle were promoted.

The end of the journey? This was Newcastle. Hardly.

Three days later, officers from Her Majesty's Revenue & Customs knocked on the Gosforth home of MD Charnley before 6am to arrest him in connection with a probe into historic transfers. Newcastle agonised about points deductions and punishments but a complex case remains ongoing. There was never any prospect of sporting sanctions that would ruin Benitez's season.

On the training ground, there was black humour. Benitez received a text from a friend saying the police were coming for him next. He replied that the transfers being discussed were from before his time. His phone lit up again: 'They're coming to arrest you for daylight robbery for getting £30m for Sissoko!'

They could laugh, but the investigation was proof that little runs smoothly on Tyneside. The Champagne was barely flat before a new set of questions to navigate. Charnley was de-arrested and released without charge. The investigation continues. Exhausted, he did not travel to Cardiff City a day later.

Benitez drew the players together and called for renewed focus. Brighton had also been promoted and needed just one more win for the title, but Benitez told his team that they were still playing for top spot. The Seagulls' defeat at Norwich before Newcastle's win against Preston spoke of a team who were distracted. Benitez's team won again, in Wales, on April 28. The gap was down to a point and it was Brighton's turn to feel the pressure.

A day later, at the AMEX, they hired an opera singer and had the trophy in the bowels of the stadium for their game against a Bristol City side who needed a victory to guarantee their Championship survival. It was set up for a coronation. The triumphant final flourish for the Seagulls? It was not to be. Hughton's men choked and lost 1-0. The scene was duly set for the final Sunday of the season. Newcastle's relentlessness – a trait Benitez had worked on from the moment they went down – had given them a title chance.

19. The Final Day

How Newcastle's Perfect Day Played Out

"Physically, the team is fine but when we get close to the box sometimes, you can see that anxiety is a problem. We must solve that"

Rafa Benitez, April 2017

9.30am: Before the buzz of the final day, there is other pressing business to attend to. There are a few fans milling around Newcastle's city centre but otherwise it feels quiet. Bill Corcoran is one of the volunteers setting up the stand for the Newcastle United Foodbank – a new initiative for the season, set up by fans' groups to support families in crisis in the city's West End.

It shouldn't need to exist but it does. And it has really helped. They estimate 750 families have had hot meals thanks to the generosity of fans donating food and money. It is football making a difference and they have been here for nearly every home match in 2017. The club has supported it since the turn of the year: Isaac Hayden visited the food bank, Rafa Benitez lent his support. Another example of the club growing from the grassroots.

The fans have responded: 3.2 tonnes of dry food were donated before the Derby match, 2.3 tonnes for the Bristol City game. These donations keep the food bank running for a week.

Alesha Aljeffri, the head of the West End foodbank, says: "It's put a buzz through the city. People have been so, so generous. It's been amazing how the fans have pulled together."

They make over a thousand pounds on the final day. Supporters stuff £20 notes in the buckets being rattled outside the stadium. The food bank will endure over the summer period, when the games stop. They have raised enough money to open a pop-up in the city's Grainger Market.

10.30am: The furious whir of helicopter blades as the private flight hugs the coastline is significant: Mike Ashley is going to be in town. He is accompanied by his ex-wife Linda on the journey, taking a trip to Tyneside for a final day that will surely not ape the bittersweet euphoria of the last two seasons.

At the ground, news of Ashley's visit was kept from most. There is no place set for the owner and he had only confirmed his presence the night before. The lounges will be packed – some of the hospitality staff are being rewarded for their hard work with a party and karaoke. It is another nice touch at a club that is starting to do things the right way.

After landing, Ashley and his partner get into a car to head into the heart of the city. Newcastle United's owner had wanted to keep it low-key. To keep the day about the team, not the regime. He has not been at St James' Park to watch a match all season but he will be there for the Barnsley match.

At St James' Park, the gates are open. It's cold and overcast – so grey that the stadium's floodlights blink into life. In the corner, volunteers from Gallowgate Flags are putting the final touches to their last display of their first season. The city feels calm but the buzz is building.

10.45am: The final teamsheet of the season is handed in. There is a reassuring familiarity about Benitez's system and formation. Everyone knows how Newcastle set up now. Player of the Season Ciaran Clark misses out through injury. Isaac Hayden replaces him on the right-hand side of the centre of defence. Aleksandar Mitrovic has an opportunity to start up front while Dwight Gayle is on the substitutes' bench.

11.40am: A few final words in the dressing room from Benitez. He emphasises that the players must enjoy the experience. It is their day, they have worked for it and have earned the acclaim that will come at the end of the match. Jamaal Lascelles will not play, but the captain is in there too, offering fist bumps and handshakes. The leader's presence is appreciated. This is a group that has grown together. The tension of Easter has disappeared. The quiet confidence is back.

11.52am: The team filter into the corridor alongside their opponents from Barnsley. Their goalkeeper, Adam Davies, spots Paul Dummett, an international colleague. There's a handshake. Rob Elliot – recalled for the final three games – carries his son Max out in his arms. He has a jersey on his back that reads 'Daddy' with his number 21. It's a poignant moment – Max was supposed to be the mascot for Newcastle's game against Crystal Palace a year before, but Elliot's season – by then – was over. Of all the things that hurt him over the course of his year out injured, missing out on that memory was the lowest moment.

Benitez follows shortly afterwards, as he always does. Deep in conversation with Mikel Antia and Antonio Gomez Perez. The work never stops.

12pm: The Gallowgate Flags' surfer flag snakes across the giant home end. The noise rumbles from four stands of St James' Park. The message from Benitez before the game was that the title did not matter, that Newcastle's season should be celebrated as a success, whatever happens. But no-one is under any illusions about what they have come hoping to see. The ovation that greets the players and Benitez is tremendous.

12.04pm: Hayden's afternoon – and season – looks to be over. Defending a Barnsley corner, he gets shoved in the back and collides, head first, with Elliot. He's down on the ground, groggy for seven minutes. He wants to play on, to be part of Newcastle history. It's typical of the attitude that has become the philosophy of the players. He is only able to last another five minutes before sitting down in the middle of the pitch, disoriented. "I wanted to carry on but things were blurry," he said. "There was no point in carrying on."

12.05pm: Quietly, and without much fuss, Ashley slips into his seat next to Lee Charnley. When he attends St James' Park, he always leaves it until the last minute to take his place in the stands. Usually, he'll have a quick drink at the bar before taking his seat. He's relaxed.

12.24pm: A Newcastle opening goal of the highest quality. Christian Atsu finds the advancing DeAndre Yedlin, who sweeps a cross into the path of Ayoze Perez. His body is twisting away from the goal but he flicks it past Davies with his right heel. A moment of Premier League ingenuity.

12.30pm: Even in the age of the smartphone and 4G signals, you cannot escape the 'ghost goal'. A roar goes around St James' Park. Someone in the crowd has got wind of a supposed Aston Villa strike against title-rivals Brighton. It is a cruel trick. Villa are holding their own, but it's goalless.

12.52pm: Half-time. Newcastle are ahead but they're reliant on Aston Villa holding out against Brighton. Through the week, Newcastle's Ciaran Clark has been texting his old friends in the second city to tell them what's at stake. They are managed by Steve Bruce, a former Sunderland manager but a Geordie who knows what it would mean.

Brighton haven't found a way through. Villa have been the better side in the first half. Villa Park – an arena synonymous with late-season drama for Newcastle – is the crucible of hope this time around. The fear is that a Brighton goal would prompt a brittle Villa to collapse.

Benitez is delighted with how the Barnsley game is going. His only request is for more of the same.

1.21pm: Chancel Mbemba doubles the home advantage. Newcastle, confident, swarming Barnsley, are applying the pressure. Ayoze Perez forces a fantastic save from Davies but Mbemba – reborn in the final weeks of the season – sweeps the loose ball into the back of the net.

1.23pm: News filters through of a Brighton penalty at Villa Park. Home defender Nathan Baker has been sent off for a foul on Sam Baldock. Glenn Murray's successful spot-kick dampens the atmosphere at St James' Park.

Newcastle remain relentless in their pressure on Barnsley. They are a world away from the constricted performances of March and April. Benitez tells his coaching team afterwards that this is the team he recognises. Now the pressure is off them, they are playing freely.

1.24pm: High in the Gods in the Leazes End, Barnsley fans sing in honour of Brighton's goal. The cheers of the visiting fans prompt defiance from the home supporters, who unite to sing: "We are going up."

1.37pm: Jonjo Shelvey's afternoon is over. Benitez withdraws him to a standing ovation from the crowd. A Newcastle career that was drifting has righted. Shelvey heads straight down the tunnel, kicks off his boots and waits for news from Villa Park.

1.39pm: On the bench, Benitez chides substitute goalkeeper Karl Darlow for checking his phone for news from Aston Villa. It is against club rules to have your phone on the bench but, like the rest of the ground, he is scrambling for a signal to find out what is going on in Birmingham. It remains 1-0 to Brighton.

1.41pm: Dwight Gayle replaces Ayoze Perez. "Two up front," Benitez tells him in the course of detailed instructions on the sideline. Newcastle will go for it in the final minutes of the Championship season. Ten minutes for the front two that Benitez had resisted playing all season. The short blanket has been discarded for the last chapter of this season.

1.51pm: An anti-climax? St James' Park feels remarkably flat, given that the game was billed as a celebration. The mood is lifted when Gayle's rapier instincts bring up Newcastle's 100th goal across all competitions. Mitrovic heads on and Gayle, with the outside of his boot, plants the ball beyond Davies.

1.52pm: Jack Grealish typifies the sort of dormant potential that

Aston Villa haven't been able to galvanise this season. There is a dividing line between talent and application and the Championship has brutally found Villa out. Two managers, £55m spent but still they have flattered to deceive over a bruising campaign. Their failings are a stark contrast to the way Rafa Benitez has managed his squad, squeezing so much out of a group that has channelled its energy towards promotion.

Yet Grealish has a crucial role to play in Newcastle's story. Brighton are a man up but failing to make that advantage count. There are seconds to go and they're hanging on. Grealish turns in the box and fires a rasping low drive. David Stockdale – born in Darlington, the Championship's Goalkeeper of the Season who chided those who had written Brighton off as "bottlers" after they achieved promotion – dives early. Grealish's deflected shot bounces over his body and ripples the net. The most important goal of the day.

At St James' Park, news filters through instantly. The players are returning to the halfway line when the guttural roar envelops the stadium. Arguably the loudest cheer of the season is for a goal 200 miles away. The 4G signal has virtually cut out now but news of the goal starts out in the suites, where the Championship scores are being shown on TVs, and spreads through the ground. Their dream scenario is playing out and the reaction is unrestrained, unconfined joy. No-one is saying the title doesn't matter now.

1.53pm: The stadium's tunnel is now packed. The atmosphere around the ground crackles with anticipation. Every single player who has featured for Newcastle has been invited to pitchside for the post-match celebrations. Benitez wanted this to be a collective effort and it has been, so they will salute the fans as one at the end. Clark is on the phone to a friend at Villa Park, getting second-by-second updates. The players are crowding around the coaching staff's iPad, waiting for news.

1.54pm: The final whistle. Newcastle have won 3-0. A comprehensive home win. Newcastle's home record – the talk of Tyneside when they drew with Bristol City in February – has carried them to the title. Another problem quietly solved.

1.56pm: Confirmation from Villa Park of Brighton's 1-1 draw. Newcastle, improbably, are champions. Atsu races towards the touchline. Lascelles and Clark bounce. A players' huddle collapses into a pile of bodies. When they do get up, the band of brothers link arms and chant 'Champions'. Hugs, high-fives everywhere.

Benitez breaks free from the celebrations among the coaching staff to seek out the players and, one-by-one, he shakes them by their hand and congratulates them. Even in the celebrations, he wants to emphasise the value of the collective. "I was not aware of the Brighton result until everyone started celebrating," he says later, with a wry smile. "But you could see everyone smiling. I said that promotion was all that matters. But that was for everyone at the club."

2.11pm: Bob Moncur, the last man to lift a major trophy with Newcastle, is the person entrusted with bringing the Football League trophy out to the hastily-constructed stage.

It is an appropriate call from the Newcastle powers-that-be. Moncur, appointed to the board as an experienced football man when Steve McClaren took the job, had taken some criticism for his relationship with Ashley over the previous season. But the reaction to the former Newcastle captain is uplifting.

He is a gentleman – well-liked and conciliatory. Adored by those who work inside the club, who admired the bravery he has shown battling and defeating cancer. He has Newcastle's best interests at heart and the criticism of the previous season was a symbol of how poor decisions had created schisms within the club. But here the response is rousing and Moncur appeared genuinely moved by it.

First on to the stage is Benitez. He has won the Champions League, the Europa League and two titles in Spain but the medal placed around his neck looks as if it means as much as any of them. He takes a look at it, grasps it in his right palm and with his left hand points his finger at the crowd. The message is clear: "This is for you."

The players are called, one-by-one and by alphabetical order, on to the stage. They take selfies and videos on the stage. Jack Colback pulls a strained, funny expression. Benitez had found social media a hindrance at Real: here his players were using it to chronicle a very modern title celebration.

2.17pm: Lascelles hasn't played but he's on the stage. Vice-captain Shelvey also has his hands on the trophy – a replica of the oldest piece of silverware in sport. This is the 'Old Lady', the trophy lifted by the great Liverpool of the eighties and part of English sporting history.

Matt Ritchie and Ciaran Clark are the first to break ranks, hopping off the stage to spray their team-mates with Champagne. Benitez tries to remain in the background, allowing the players to take the shine. But he is caught by Gayle's bottle of Champagne, which soaks his suit jacket. The smile suggests he doesn't mind. Lascelles plants a kiss on the trophy.

2.21pm: These are the celebrations of the champions. Children, wives, girlfriends and families on the pitch, soaking in the adulation of a crowd who have taken these players to their hearts. The dysfunction and divides of previous years dissolved.

"Dad, dad!" Clark holds the trophy by one hand, seeking out his father in the press box. Mbemba, Yedlin and Anita take selfies with the trophy. Shelvey has won an England cap and played at Anfield, but this looks like one of the moments of his career.

There's a lap of honour. Every single supporter stays to applaud.

Benitez and his coaching team hang a bit further back, allowing the players to take centre stage.

Hayden's concussion is not serious. He is cleared to celebrate with the rest of the team. "We got a bit lucky," he admits.

"It was football in a nutshell. Things happen – they can go your way, they might not. Today, they went our way, and it's a fantastic day, especially for the fans. It's good to have the last game at home, and to win it like we did was fabulous."

2.36pm: Benitez walks into the press suite, his suit jacket is still damp from the Champagne. The medal hangs around his neck. He is beaming. So, how was it? The manager, softened by age, gets sentimental.

"I don't have the English words to describe what happened. It's difficult to say because I have been a manager for so many years but you appreciate it more when you get older, and you feel the emotion around the city and the stadium and everywhere.

"I would like to dedicate the title to everyone involved – the staff, the players, the fans, everyone.

"Thank you to all of them. I said before that we had to come with a smile on our faces, and maybe go back home with an even bigger smile.

"I am really proud of these players, of everyone. You can see and feel that the fans were very emotional."

How did it compare to the final game of the previous season, when Benitez was famously love-bombed into submission by Newcastle's fans?

"It was the same as the last game of the last season, but in a different way. It was much better."

Was it important that Ashley, already enjoying a bottle of beer in a celebratory chairman's suite, was there?

"I already have an idea of what a successful club could look like. I think, also, he has an idea."

And, with that, Benitez gets up and walks out to a standing ovation from the press pack.

2.45pm: The stadium's empty barring a group of 20 or so fans having their picture taken with a huge flag in the Gallowgate End. Friends and family are at the bar, drinking. They have given their own time to collect the flags that their group raised money and paid for. The Gallowgate Flags group were here before everyone, and they're here after everyone, too.

3.30pm: Benitez has emerged from the dressing room. He takes the lift to the chairman's suite and has his hands on the trophy. Ashley is posing for pictures: firstly with Charnley, then all three of them. There's a meaty handshake. People are taking pictures of them. Whatever issues there were in the depths of mid-winter have been swept away by the emotion of the day.

When Benitez is spotted in the lounges, there is a huge roar. People are cheering, clapping. The manager is mobbed.

"Rafa!" says Ashley, greeting Benitez. Congratulations, warm words exchanged. For those watching in the chairman's suite, hope. Pictures crop up on social media. Nerves over what comes next are soothed.

The first phase of the Rafalution is over but Benitez wants to get the second stage rolling. They'll talk again soon. To those watching in, there is a feeling that Ashley – smiling – gets what the club can be if it continues to work like this. Those who speak to him hear talk of the future, of what it would be like if Newcastle won a major trophy. It feels like Benitez has fired an enthusiasm in him. The drinking and singing goes on long into the night.

4.30pm: Finally, Benitez leaves the stadium. Supporters are still milling around the entrance. He poses for every picture with fans, signs a few programmes. The job has been done.

***

TWENTY-FOUR hours later, Benitez is back at St James' Park. The Champagne has been drunk, the hangovers still lingering. This time there are only a few hundred in the stadium, the hardy souls who watch every single kick of the season. Friends, family and supporters who want to see the under-23 team in their play-off semi-final with Fulham.

Benitez visits the dressing room before the game kicks-off to wish the young players luck, then takes his seat in the stands. Antonio Gomez Perez is there with him. Simon Smith is watching Matz Sels, whose form has seen him fall down the pecking order.

Newcastle win 2-0. Under-23 manager Peter Beardsley thinks Benitez's presence made the difference. Another small victory for the details man, to go with Sunday's restorative triumph.

Epilogue

"I think I know what a successful club could look like"

Rafa Benitez, May 2017

THE whir of helicopter blades again. This time over Benton; this time they carried the hopes of Newcastle United fans with them.

Mike Ashley was back in town just 48 hours after Newcastle had confirmed their title win. His helicopter ride from London was the most anticipated journey of the summer. Tyneside lived in hope: losing their transformative manager was the scenario that troubled fans from the point in January when he subtly reminded the powers-that-be that his patience was not eternal.

Benitez told the BBC's *Football Focus* in the week before the final game that he could envisage himself staying at Newcastle for a decade – if everything fell into place as he hoped it would. But there were conditions on his loyalty, and he wanted a chance to sell his vision to Ashley.

***

BENITEZ arrived in the North East with a reputation that was ambushed by his time in charge at Real Madrid. He had been left frustrated by the egos of the Bernabeu and bruised by the briefings. He was accused of standing out of touch with the rise of the superstar footballer.

For all that Newcastle needed Benitez, he too had to make the right choice if he was coming back to the Premier League. A return to England was what he wanted, but another bruising experience like the one at Chelsea? The conflict was draining. For a man who approaches football as meticulously as Benitez does, it was important that his next choice allowed him to manage the way that he wanted.

Newcastle was the right club at the right time for Benitez. Its dysfunction had brought it to a crossroads. Lee Charnley had spoken about making Newcastle the best it could be "pound for pound" but that philosophy appeared cold and charmless. It had brought nothing but frustration, widening the schism between supporters and their club. Benitez brought his way of working to Newcastle: the philosophy and beliefs that had been honed ever since he started beating his brother in those back garden games of Stratego in the hot summer sun in Madrid.

What he did at Newcastle was manage so much more than just the free-kicks, corners and training sessions. Benitez realised that managing Newcastle meant being in charge of everything. Mending everything. Most importantly, it meant including everyone.

The phrase 'Rafalution' implies laying waste to all that went before, uprooting what was there and replacing it with something new. But what Benitez discovered at Newcastle was people who wanted to improve, who found themselves held back by the divide between the club and its people. Bridging that was the key to turning Newcastle United around.

EPILOGUE

When he first agreed to lead the Championship salvage mission, there were people who wondered if he was the right man for a season among the muck and nettles of English football's second tier. Some saw a man with limited experience at that level and figured that he would take too long to recalibrate his management and scouting expertise with what was required in a division that is less technical, and more physical, than he is used to.

But they underestimated Benitez's work ethic. That summer he hit the phones, spoke to agents, spoke to players and listened to every bit of advice that he was given about life in the Championship. It informed plans which paid off in the final minute of the season in a joyous denouement.

There was a moment after the trophy had been hoisted on the final day when Benitez had it in his possession. He took a look around the empty stadium and drank in the moment. The smile barely left his lips. He had arrived at Newcastle with the reputation of being cold, analytical and ruthless. But at Newcastle he had shown himself to be anything but.

At that point the penny dropped. Benitez would not walk away from this. Not while there was still so much to be done.

***

IN four hours, Ashley talked to Benitez about the summer to come. Benitez spoke of changes in personnel, of funds that would be required. He agreed that the business model had to make sense. He wanted to know whether the owner understood what was required to keep growing the club.

In his first summer he had wanted to change the mood of the training ground with the stroke of a paintbrush. In the years to come, something more fundamental would have to happen. A training-ground upgrade was overdue. Newcastle would have to keep growing and keep thinking big.

The one thing that people who have witnessed his work all agree with is that Benitez always wants more. He always wants better. Ashley consented. The meeting broke up positively. It felt like a big moment in Newcastle's history. The Rafalution would roll on. You get the feeling that if it is up to him, it has barely begun.

After promotion was achieved, Benitez was asked what comes next. His answer? Simple. Improvement. "You have to change things and try to improve.

"When you achieve something and then start preparing for the next challenge, you have to be excited. I'm thinking about every single detail I can improve."

It was this drive that had helped piece a shattered club back together, given supporters prepared to write off their passion a vision of what it might be. Of all the things that Benitez delivered – for all the talk of a revolution – it was allowing people to believe and dream that was his greatest gift to Newcastle United.